A D
SHITTY SALES

"Adam cuts through the bullshit and shows you exactly what it takes to be a great leader."

—**TUCKER MAX,** author of *New York Times* #1 best seller *I Hope They Serve Beer in Hell*

"I've had the privilege of working with some exceptional leaders in my career and I put Adam in that category. Truly effective sales leadership takes a combination of grit, authenticity, doing hard things, and showing up for your team. *Shitty Sales Leaders: And How to Not Be One* should be required reading for all sales leaders, regardless of their tenure. Adam has taken what could be a dry subject and provided a personal, authentic, touching, and humorous template for sales leaders to level up their game and drive world-class results."

—**DAN FITZSIMONS,** Chief Revenue Officer, Pure Storage

"I'm delighted that Adam wrote this book! So many people go about leadership the wrong way, and Adam nailed what it takes to be an effective, inclusive, and inspirational leader. He shared specific examples from his personal journey and the key attributes of the greatest leaders. If you want an authentic, touching, sincere guide to success, read this book!"

—**RIMA ALAMEDDINE**, Vice President Sales, Nvidia

"As someone that did not grow up around salespeople or sales leaders, Adam's book is a refreshing take on what a good sales leader is and is not, and how, with a plan and dedication, you too can become a great sales leader. A fantastic new approach to an old profession by a true renaissance sales leader."

—**BILL KOHUT**, Senior Vice President, Cisco

"Adam captures what it takes to be an effective leader, and Adam embodies what it means to be a great leader. Read this book, seek your inspiration, make these lessons your own, find your fuel, and become the greatest leader you can be."

—**MARK NIEMIEC**, Senior Vice President, Salesforce

"Some of us are lucky and have had a chance to work with great leaders. I would wager everyone has worked for and with a shitty leader (or two or three). But there is only one Adam Apps: the most observant and thoughtful leader I've ever worked with. Adam is a lifelong learner, both a great student and a great teacher. He has a value system you will align with and a style that is direct, funny, and easy to relate to. In this book, he has taken the time to share his journey and distill the lessons he's internalized. I highly recommend you read the book and highly recommend you connect with and get to know Adam!"

—**PETE AGRESTA**, Vice President, Enterprise Sales, Pure Storage

"The best leaders I know are never too busy to send a thank you note or acknowledge your message. The best leaders I know have high levels of self-awareness and genuine empathy for their team. In this book, Adam has captured the core essence of great sales leaders in a manner that is anything but dry, boring, and trite. I read this book in one sitting on a plane while heading to a business trip, and I mentioned to my team right after that we should make this a book we all read and share best practices from. Whether you are new to leadership or have had the opportunity to serve as a leader for a while, Adam's book gives you concrete tools to remind you that not only are great sales leaders kind, thoughtful, and caring; they are among the most effective when it comes to consistently building top-performing teams and gaining followership."

—**ANUJA SINGH**, Solutions Architecture Leader, Amazon Web Services

"Adam is one of those unique sales leaders who manage to lead teams with empathy and humanity while still setting a high standard of excellence, accountability, and execution. His approach to leadership shows that a rising tide truly does lift all boats. In *Shitty Sales Leaders: And How to Not Be One*, Adam eloquently details why, in today's war for top talent, the tired and dated SSL approach of 'the beatings will continue until morale and numbers improve' must be replaced with a more positive, uplifting, innovative, motivating, and authentic approach to leading people and teams in order for organizations to attract, grow, and retain the top performers required to win."

—**JEFF DISTASIO**, Sales Director, Google

"The most effective sales leaders make it look easy, but in actuality it's really difficult. It's a muscle that needs to be exercised every day. I've worked with hundreds of sales leaders in my career and Adam just 'gets it.' In this book, Adam provides a framework for achieving high levels of performance and shines a light on the attributes shared by the most inspirational and effective leaders—authenticity, empathy, and hard work!"

—**ANDREW MARTIN**, Vice President & General Manager, Americas Sales, Pure Storage

"I agree, leadership and sales leadership can be and are learned over time and learned across multiple aspects of your life. Some people may have natural ability but life-long learning, humility, and confidence are keys to becoming a great sales leader. It is more about what people think and feel about you than what you think about yourself."

—**KEVIN DELANE**, Chief Revenue Officer, Cohesity

SALES
LEADERS

AND HOW TO *NOT* BE ONE

ADAM APPS

FOREWORD WRITTEN BY
DAVID "HAT" HATFIELD

HOUNDSTOOTH
PRESS

SHITTY SALES LEADERS
And How to Not Be One

ISBN 978-1-5445-3443-5 *Hardcover*
      978-1-5445-3442-8 *Paperback*
      978-1-5445-3441-1 *Ebook*

For my wife, Meredith,
and my son, Adam George.

CONTENTS

DISCLAIMER

This publication contains the opinions and ideas of its author. It is sold with the understanding that the author is not engaged in rendering professional advice or services. The strategies outlined in this book may not be suitable for every individual or situation, and are not guaranteed or warranted to produce any particular results. The author specifically disclaims any responsibility for any liability, loss, or risk that is incurred as a consequence, directly or indirectly, of the use or application of any of the contents of this book.

FOREWORD

by David "Hat" Hatfield, Co-Chief Executive Officer, Lacework

When I reflect back on my journey from sales rep to CEO, I am humbled and grateful for the number of leaders who have contributed to my development and provided a template for excellence.

Most leaders, including myself, fall victim to common pitfalls. We are confronted with obstacles that seem insurmountable in the moment. The road to leadership is fraught with perils but if you know where to look, it is also paved with invaluable lessons and opportunities. If I could encapsulate the key learnings from my journey and go back in time, I would hand my younger self a copy of this book.

Sales leadership is a uniquely challenging endeavor for the reasons Adam outlines. Countless studies and books have been written on the topic of sales leadership and most tend to be dry, boring, or self-aggrandizing. This book has a unique and fresh perspective on the topic.

Adam shares lessons from his inspirational leadership journey in a captivating and relatable way that makes you want to read until the end. Through real-world examples and actionable advice, the reader is left with a guidebook they can put to immediate use in their own career.

Many people in sales would agree that they/we can be distracted easily, making it even harder for folks like us to commit the time needed to get through any book, let alone one about sales leadership. Fortunately, *Shitty Sales Leaders: And How to Not Be One* is written in plain language, which makes for an easy, fast, and enjoyable read.

Adam's observations about what makes great leaders so effective are rarely discussed. The best sales leaders are not always the alpha, and in many cases, that profile can be the worst or most shitty, as Adam outlines. Anyone can lead if they have empathy, genuine curiosity in other people, and sincere interest in helping them achieve their personal and professional goals...and a willingness to put in the work to help make it happen.

Adam captures the essence of servant leadership and recognizes that authentic leadership is not innate—it can be learned—and some of the best I've worked with got there not because they were the loudest in the room, but because they cared the most and put the work in.

I am confident that everyone who reads this book will take away a new lesson for their arsenal, regardless of where they are on their leadership journey.

I've personally worked with Adam and witnessed him implement the practices he lays out in this book with tremendous results. Adam's authentic voice and humility can be heard throughout this book and he provides you with a chronological and actionable template to up level your leadership game and have a long-lasting positive impact on your team.

NATURAL LEADERS

How do you identify a leader? We have been told, "Leaders stand out; you feel their presence, they exude confidence, and they are frequently the loudest voice in the room." These individuals are supposedly the "natural leaders" among us, a category in which only ten percent of people find themselves.[1] But what if we have it all wrong when it comes to identifying the most effective people to lead sales teams?

In the pages that follow, we examine real-world examples where "natural leaders" are ineffective as sales leaders. You will discover that some of the most effective and

---

1   Beck, Randall J., and Jim Harter, "Why Great Managers Are So Rare," Gallup, October 22, 2018, https://www.gallup.com/workplace/231593/why-great-managers-rare.aspx.

beloved sales leaders possess common, nontraditional characteristics that are rarely attributed to "natural leaders," and I provide actionable steps you can take toward becoming a great leader.

The people we generally consider to be the "natural leaders" among us are often deficient when it comes to effectively leading sales teams for a multitude of reasons that I examine in this book. Despite their deficiencies, these ineffective people continue to be hired and promoted into sales leadership roles, which begs the question, "How do the rest of us who aren't necessarily the loudest voice in the room land these leadership roles and break the cycle?"

In this book, I challenge the notion that only ten percent of people can lead. I cite evidence that, when armed with the right tools and motivation, anybody can be an effective sales leader. Furthermore, I discuss why "natural leaders" are often detrimental to the performance and development of a sales team. I propose we reevaluate the attributes we seek in our sales leaders and we examine why the loudest voice in the room is usually not the right person to lead and inspire a sales team on a long-term basis. I will discuss how you can make your voice heard, become an uncontested leadership candidate, land leadership jobs, and have a positive, long-lasting impact on your teams through your career in leadership.

Followers rely on their leaders, and leaders rely on their followers. Leading and following is a symbiotic relationship that exists to diminish individual risk and enhance group prosperity. Consider the notion often attributed to Aristotle and later in German Gestalt psychology that "the whole is greater than the sum of its parts."[2] The primary role of a leader is to motivate a group (the whole) toward a goal or achievement that is greater than the individual (the parts) by understanding and nurturing the motivations of both the individual and the group.

Our cave-dwelling ancestors are thought to have been acephalous, or existing without formally elected leaders or rulers, but it is generally agreed upon that they did have temporarily appointed leaders who were responsible for taking initiative while performing specific tasks like hunting. It makes sense that the stealthiest, most skilled hunter would lead the group on its quest for sustenance. From a survival perspective, strong leadership acts as an impediment to natural selection for the weaker members of the group and provides protection and proliferation of the species.

The intrinsic method of identifying a "natural leader" based on our most primal human needs has been key to

---

2   Aristotle, *Aristotle in 23 Volumes*, trans. Hugh Tredennick (Cambridge, MA: Harvard University Press; London: William Heinemann Ltd., 1933, 1989), vol. 17, 18.

our survival for thousands of years. Imagine for a moment you find yourself shipwrecked on a deserted island with ten strangers. A "natural leader" quickly emerges. More than likely, the leader is the physically strongest person who can secure food, build shelter, find fresh water, make a fire, fend off predators, delegate tasks, maintain social order, and generally keep everyone alive and comfortable.

Here's the tricky part: the strong leader who keeps you safe and warm on the island might not be the same leader you need to get you off the island. Put differently, what got you here won't get you there.

The leader who gets you off the island is somebody you would willingly follow into an uncertain or dangerous situation, a person upon whom the majority of the group agrees is best suited to lead them out of danger and into a more stable and secure situation. If your newly entrusted island leader sees a boat on the horizon and tells the group it's time to swim toward it, you need to feel very comfortable with the leader's critical thinking skills and ability to assess risk before jumping into the cold, shark-infested waters. Moreover, if you doubt your own ability to swim safely to the boat, you need a leader who believes in you more than you believe in yourself, somebody who pushes you to do things beyond what you consider possible. You need a leader who knows how to motivate and inspire you toward a successful outcome.

Similarly, the leader who gets you off the island might not be the same leader you need to establish long-term prosperity after you reach the mainland. To ensure ongoing growth and development, you need a selfless and thoughtful leader who puts your needs first, an authentic leader with real experience who can guide, coach, and motivate you. This leader is not necessarily the same "natural leader" identified the day you shipwrecked on the island.

Clearly, different scenarios call for different styles of leadership. Leaders need to pivot and adapt to fluid situations, and in some cases, entirely different leaders are needed to ensure successful outcomes.

Humans aren't the only ones who rely on strong natural leaders to ensure safety and survival. Just look at the animal world. Wolf packs are led by male and female breeding pairs whose responsibilities include procreating the species and leading the hunt for prey—and the breeding pairs are often the first to eat. Chimpanzee communities rally around strong alpha males and have been known to follow their leaders into violent battles against rival communities.[3] Even insects rely on leaders for survival. Australian

3 Lincoln Park Zoo, "Nature of war: Chimps inherently violent; Study disproves theory that 'chimpanzee wars' are sparked by human influence," ScienceDaily, September 17, 2014, https://www.sciencedaily.com/releases/2014/09/140917131816.htm

caterpillar larvae have been observed following their leaders on life-sustaining, food-foraging expeditions,[4] and bees rely on their queen to unite and direct them via chemical emissions, without which entire hives fall into chaos and cease to exist.

Historically, corporations have hired and promoted "natural leaders" using the same techniques as our chimpanzee cousins. Sometimes, these "natural leaders" are considered to be very effective, and they might even produce short-term results. Other times, these "natural leaders" are simply the loudest voices in the room who talked their way into leadership roles through brute force. These people might find themselves in positions of leadership, but having a leadership title does not make one a leader. True leadership requires no title at all.

Leadership principles are universally applicable, regardless of industry, or vertical, because they are based on human behaviors and motivations. However, to maximize your effectiveness as a leader in a sales environment, you require more than just basic leadership competence. The composition, desires, and motivations of sales teams are very unique, therefore, sales teams require a unique and

4   Hodgkin L.K., M.R. Symonds, M.A. Elgar. "Leaders benefit followers in the collective movement of a social sawfly." *Proceedings of the Royal Society B* 281, no. 1796 (2014):20141700. doi: 10.1098/rspb.2014.1700.

thoughtful leadership approach to realize their full potential.

Sales representatives (reps) are part of an exclusive club. They generally did not go to school to prepare for a career in sales, although some colleges now offer majors in sales. Most people find themselves in sales because they lack specialized talents or interests. If you are passionate about marine biology and have the aptitude required for a successful career in that field, then you will likely take all the necessary steps to become a marine biologist. The same could be said for other specialized fields, like accounting, marketing, nursing, and so on. But for the rest of us, our passions were not as apparent; we needed a little extra time to find something that ignited our inner spark. We might have floundered in college (if we went to college—plenty of salespeople didn't), trying out different majors or part-time jobs to find our niche. For better or worse and through trial and error, we found ourselves making a living in sales.

I am not unique. My sales career started rather unintentionally. As I approached the date of my college graduation, I told my career counselor I would be interested in looking at *any* career path, except for sales. My impression of salespeople was not a good one. The word "salesperson" immediately brought to mind a fast-talking used car salesman employing underhanded tactics and trickery to convince people to part with their hard-earned money. At the advice of my career counselor, I took a personality and aptitude test; the results kept pointing me toward a career in sales. Having no other specialized talent or interests and faced with limited options, I decided to broaden my search to include a career in sales.

There is no shortage of sales positions available for recent college graduates. A significant element of a sales representative's compensation is tied to individual performance. The sales generated by a sales rep contribute to a company's top-line revenue and profitability, so sales is typically an area in which companies are willing to invest.

In bear markets, companies invest in their sales force to boost revenue. In bull markets, companies invest in their sales force to increase profitability and fend off the competition. Sales, therefore, is a relatively recession-proof career path where jobs are usually plentiful. Companies realize that for a relatively low cost and high return, a well-staffed, high-performing sales force is a vital component of go-to market strategies.

The direct correlation between a salesperson's performance and the salesperson's individual work ethic tends to attract gritty, self-starter types. We would rather bet on our own ability than rely on somebody else to put food on our table. Individuals who have chosen to make a living in sales are demonstrating strength, personal accountability, and entrepreneurial bravery by wagering on their ability to deliver results in a crowded, competitive, and often adversarial environment.

If we accept that sales representatives are brave and accountable, based on the choice to make a living in sales, then they should be considered leaders in their own right who require a different kind of motivation and leadership. The highest-performing sales reps are often viewed as difficult to manage or as having a chip on their shoulder for a reason. These individuals are not "clock punchers"—they are entrepreneurial, self-motivated, highly compensated professionals with a unique set of motivations and desires who view themselves as the only key to their success. They are harder on themselves than anyone else can be, and they have only themselves to blame or credit when things go wrong or right. It's clear to see why a traditional management approach does not work with these people—they won't tolerate it.

Motivating and managing *individuals* is only part of the role of a leader. Putting a group of sales reps together as a team creates a new dynamic (or a mob mentality, depending on your vantage point) that presents its own set of challenges. I like to compare a sales team to a car engine made up of many components. Each component needs specialized care, like oil, fluid, grease, or coolant, but the engine as a whole needs fuel to reach its destination. Understanding and nurturing an individual's needs, quirks, and desires while fueling the overall team with coaching and motivation is a balancing act that requires a chameleon-like approach.

Another variable that sales leaders must account for is the maturity of their teams. If the team is in its infancy and just getting started, a very different leadership approach is needed to achieve short-term results and long-term growth than that needed for an already established veteran sales team.

Acquiring, building, and running high-performing sales teams requires a carefully calibrated, results-driven leadership style based upon three core principles: Accountability, Recognition, and Consistency (which we will discuss in Chapter 7). Unfortunately, the current method of hiring and promoting sales leaders is deeply rooted. As a result, you have likely worked for a bad manager in your sales career who just doesn't "get it." You know who these managers are. We've all worked for them. They are the "shitty sales leaders" who inspired this book. I use the word "shitty" because it is a suitably strong enough word to capture my emotion on the subject. Shitty sales leaders can ruin careers, scare great people away from leadership opportunities, and destroy team cultures, company reputations, and entire industries.

The only thing worse than a shitty sales leader ruining somebody's professional life by creating a toxic work environment is for that leader to allow the toxicity to spill over into people's personal lives, adversely impacting spouses and children, which is...pretty shitty.

Shitty sales leaders might deliver short-term results at the expense of those around them, but their approach is never sustainable. Either their teams will band together and force them out, or team members will choose to leave. Regardless, the shitty sales leader can't be a leader if nobody is willing to follow.

The lack of employee retention and disruption caused by shitty sales leaders forces companies to continuously reinvest and rebuild, creating operational inefficiencies and negatively impacting results. This cycle of disruption often is viewed as a normal by-product of a strong leader thinning the herd; some managers even wear it as a badge of honor and a testament to their leadership strength!

The characteristics exhibited by shitty sales leaders are endless. Typically, these people are selfish, egocentric, critical, hostile, bullies, micromanagers, coercive, intimidating, oppressive, threatening, hypocritical, idea stealers... you get the idea.

The way shitty leaders behave is not necessarily their

fault. They are probably trying to mimic what they think a strong leader looks like, maybe a boss or drill sergeant portrayed in a movie. They also, more than likely, are making up for their own deficiencies and insecurities instead of taking the time to understand the key aspects of long-term inspirational and effective leadership. They have never looked inwardly to understand why they do the things they do and to wonder if there could be a better way to inspire people to produce great results. The good news is, there is a better way!

Instead of focusing on the infinite list of things that shitty sales leaders do, this book focuses on things that shitty sales leaders *do not* do. We will spend our time and energy analyzing the positive attributes and secrets shared by all great leaders, and I promise to not use the word "shitty" gratuitously for the remainder of the book.

The world needs great leaders, but being a leader is burdensome. The leader carries the responsibility for the well-being of the group and is faced with the most difficult situations and decisions. Shakespeare captured King Henry's burden in *Henry IV, Part 2*: "Uneasy is the head that wears the crown."

Leadership isn't easy and it's not for everyone. Leadership is a privilege. When approached with thoughtfulness and care, it can be the most rewarding experience of your life. If you are honest with yourself and willing to put in the time and work, you can become the inspirational, life-changing leader whom people are searching for.

I know what it takes to be an Olympic athlete: dedication, raw talent, persistence, practice, coaching, development, nutrition, and more. But just knowing what it takes doesn't mean that I will ever find myself on an Olympic podium. I also know what it takes to be a great leader, but that doesn't mean I consider myself a great leader. In fact, I am sure I have been unwittingly shitty at some points throughout my career. Like everyone, I am a work in progress, constantly striving for greatness but often missing the mark.

I do not have all the answers. No silver bullets or magic words will make you a great leader; anyone who tells you otherwise is lying. There are some best practices and "secrets" possessed by great leaders that I share in this book, but becoming a great leader takes a culmination of experience, introspection, and constant self-improvement.

It's not lost on me that I have been dealt an unfair advantage in life. My white male privilege has opened doors that too often are shut to equally qualified and underrepresented minorities. Thus I feel a sense of obligation to help others unlock their full potential and uncover opportunities to flourish; I've been a career coach and mentor for years. I've proudly watched people go on to achieve great things and have very successful careers in sales and leadership through a combination of their own hard work and my recommendations. One of my primary motivations in writing this book is to open doors for even more people who might otherwise find them closed.

I hope the guidance and observations shared in this book are not interpreted as some guy "mansplaining" how he's such a great leader and saying, "If you work hard, just maybe you can be like me." This book is not about me. I wrote it from my point of view and my perspective because the experiences I've had and the lessons I've learned are accessible to anybody who is willing to put in the work.

Although burdensome at times, leadership can be a very rewarding endeavor. I have personally found that the return far outweighs the investment. I hope after reading this book, you will embark on your own introspective and authentic leadership journey with a renewed belief in your abilities. My desire is that you find new ways to have a positive impact on the lives of your team.

ONE

FIND YOUR FUEL

Shortly after graduating from college, I landed an interview for an entry-level sales job at a financial services firm. The company incorporated a written behavioral assessment in its screening process to help identify top candidates. All the questions in the assessment were clearly designed to identify potential leadership attributes. Questions like, "Would you rather be up on a stage or in the crowd?" I didn't know it at the time, but a lot of leadership assessments are out there, one of the most common and well-known being the MBTI, or Myers-Briggs Type Indicator®.[5] The MBTI assessment was launched in the 1960s and divides people into sixteen

---

5   Isabel Briggs Myers, *The Myers-Briggs type indicator: manual* (Palo Alto: Consulting Psychologists Press, 1962).

personality types, such as extrovert and introvert. I think a personality assessment is a worthwhile exercise and a good step toward identifying and understanding your natural tendencies, but I don't think it should be the sole determining factor in an interview setting.

The question about being up on a stage stuck with me for decades. Of course, I knew what they wanted to hear—they were looking for the stage seeker, the alpha wolf, not the crowd dweller. If I was being honest with myself, the thought of being on a literal stage was terrifying, while being in the crowd felt a lot more comfortable. I knew that if I lied, telling them I would love to be up on stage, I would probably get the job and some much-needed income. Instead, I decided to answer honestly, and unsurprisingly, I was not called back.

That interview experience haunted me. By answering the assessment honestly, I was classified as an introvert, and as far as I knew, introverts could not be leaders. But prior to taking the behavioral assessment, I always considered myself to be a natural leader. As a kid, my friends called me the leader of our group and deferred to me for plan making and tie breaking.

While in college, I got a part-time job in the campus computing department. I took as many shifts as they would give me and frequently covered for other people. I guess finding reliable workers was hard for them in a college setting where late nights and hangovers were a regular occurrence, especially for the early morning shifts. After a short time in that role, I was promoted to a leadership position as a supervisor. I managed more than fifty employees and was responsible for running training sessions and overseeing facilities in multiple locations. I recently found an "employee of the month" award from those days. My supervisor wrote:

> You might not guess it, but underneath Adam Apps' quiet exterior is a resourceful and knowledgeable consultant. Adam is a great asset to the lab as he frequently takes emergency coverage; he is respectful of lab patrons and takes their questions seriously. Although we don't hear too much from Adam's end of the room, we always know the job is well taken care of when Adam is there.

My approach to working wasn't calculated or groundbreaking. I showed up, quietly did my job to the best of my ability, and helped anyone who was struggling. I didn't seek leadership roles, but they seemed to materialize as a by-product of my effort.

My leadership style developed organically. When my team faced challenges, I tried to inspire and motivate them toward action rather than telling them what to do. I always preferred to listen to others and analyze a situation before forming an opinion and chiming in. If I thought people were not working to their full potential, I encouraged them to achieve greater things because I believed in them and thought they were capable of more. I didn't see any point in yelling at people to make them work harder; I couldn't make them want something they didn't want for themselves. I knew that barking orders likely would result in short-term performance and long-term resentment. Instead, I wanted to help people unlock their full potential, to see something in themselves that was apparent to me. I wanted to fuel their motivation.

My quiet, consultative approach to leadership could not be described as extroverted. How could I be both an introvert and a "natural leader"? Doesn't one preclude the other? Based on the behavioral assessment, I decided that some companies are explicitly looking for the loudest voice in the room, and that wasn't me.

Twenty years after I took that behavioral assessment, I found myself standing on a stage at a convention center in San Francisco at a global sales conference. I was alone in front of thousands of people, responsible for hundreds of millions of dollars in revenue, talking about the evolution of our go-to market strategy as a sales director for a leading Silicon Valley–based tech company.

The years leading up to that moment on stage were filled with thousands of interactions, decisions, and lessons. I had pushed myself to do things every single day that were stressful, difficult, uncomfortable, and generally scary, while a lot of people around me were understandably satisfied taking much easier paths. Why? Why am I constantly putting myself in uncomfortable situations? Why am I so competitive? Why am I never satisfied? Why are some people drawn to leadership?

Only when we understand our deepest motivations (our "why") and their underlying roots can we realize our full potential by fueling our inner motivation engine and accelerating our growth. Motivation is a funny thing; it can be positive or negative, and it fluctuates over time. If you eat healthy and go to the gym every day, you are motivated toward a positive outcome, a healthy and fit body. Alternatively, fear of being overweight or unhealthy is negative motivation, but it still gets you in the gym with the same end result. Negative motivation isn't a bad thing and can sometimes be stronger and more effective than positive motivation.

Motivation can fluctuate between positive and negative, for example, today you want to skip the gym and eat a cheeseburger and fries because you are lacking positive motivation to be healthy. There are degrees of motivation, too—perhaps you'll skip the fries but embrace the cheeseburger.

Understanding what impacts our motivation levels is the only way to harness them. So, how do we find the root of our motivation? The answers usually lie in our childhood and upbringing. We can debate whether leaders are born or made, but it's clear to me that our early developmental years significantly impact our motivation.

I believe that we all have the capacity to lead if we can find our deepest inner motivations. If we learn how to unlock true motivation in ourselves, we have taken the first and most important step in our leadership journey: introspection.

TWO

INTROSPECTION

ntrospection can be uncomfortable and we might not like what we find, but to know where we are going, we must first know where we came from. Taking the time to conduct a deep and honest self-examination is the first step toward achieving self-awareness, a key attribute of great leadership.

Early in my leadership career, I received some pretty direct feedback from my manager: people thought I was intense, unapproachable, and standoffish. I considered myself fairly self-aware at the time, so hearing that people had that perception of me was jarring. Apparently, I had blind spots. I needed to sit down and reflect on my "why." Why was I so intense? Why do people view me as unapproachable? Why am I this way?

When you are lost, you can find your way by retracing your steps and going back to the beginning. In the pages that follow, I share a glimpse into my own personal introspection journey, which can serve as a framework for yours. This is only a template—self-examination is a very personal matter—but I encourage you to reach deep and far to find the root of your "why." Start at the beginning, work gradually toward present day, and spend time revisiting your childhood, your family, your friends, and your colleagues. As you do so, keep in mind that you are shaped by your experiences, but you are not bound by them.

SELF-EXAMINATION

I grew up in a lower-middle-class area of London, England, called Essex. I was surrounded by a loving family, had a roof over my head, went on family holidays, and I have a lot of happy and loving memories from that time. I was more fortunate than a lot of people, but I also was surrounded by a lack of financial means. I didn't feel poor as a kid, but I knew we didn't have money to spare. Going out for dinner at a restaurant was a rare treat reserved for birthdays or other very special occasions. If we needed anything beyond the basics, we had to work for it.

I was seven years old when I got my first job. My sister and I worked together delivering newspapers around London. The newspaper company sent a truck in the morning (before the sun came up) to drop off a huge pile of newspapers, leaflets, and bags. My sister and I sat in our hallway, folded the newspapers in half, placed a leaflet inside each one, and put them in plastic bags to be delivered. We loaded up our "sholleys" (shopping trolleys) and walked door to door, pushing the newspapers through the slots. Our tiny hands turned black from newsprint, dogs barked as we approached front doors, and the cold morning mist coated our faces. I remember on one occasion I was having trouble fitting a paper through a particularly narrow slot. I used my hand to push it all the way through to the other side, and when I pulled my hand back, my knuckles got caught on the sharp metal edge and bled for the rest of the route.

As far as jobs go, delivering newspapers early in the morning wasn't the most comfortable thing in the world, but it felt good to be doing something productive, contributing to the family and serving our community. I sometimes saw people at their windows waiting for us to arrive. I took great pride in knowing that people relied on us for their morning news. Also, though the pay was minuscule, a couple of extra pounds in my pocket every month was more than enough to buy a large bag of penny sweets, back when sweets actually cost one pence each. To this day, the smell of a newspaper takes me right back to that time and place.

We lived in an attached row home where we frequently heard domestic disputes through our thin, shared walls. The neighborhood was not somewhere we felt safe walking at night; the community generally had an air of tension and despair. Seeing children physically disciplined in public places was common, and through my young eyes, people seemed depressed, downtrodden, and exhausted.

Bored, unsupervised groups of juvenile delinquents roamed aimlessly around town. The schools had no funding for after-school programs, and parents were out working to put food on the table, which left these kids to fend for themselves. As an adolescent, I regularly found myself interacting with these kids, which always seemed to end in a fistfight. I didn't go looking for trouble, but it always seemed to find me. I was shorter than most of the boys my age, so I quickly learned how to sweep my opponents' legs out from underneath them early in a fight, taking them to the ground and literally leveling the playing field.

Once, I was walking home from school and a kid jumped out of the bushes with a knife, ordering me to empty my pockets. I knew who he was. We went to school together, but he must've known that I wouldn't tell anyone because he made no attempt to hide his face. Handing over the few coins in my pocket was a small price to pay compared to the special treatment reserved for snitches. After that encounter, I started carrying a pocket knife on my walk to school, hoping I would never need to use it. Thankfully, I never did. Looking back at that time now, I can only imagine what that kid was dealing with at home to make him resort to robbery with a deadly weapon.

Living through this experience, I understand how people born into lower-income communities can easily fall into despondency and crime. Seeing a way out is hard. Many of my childhood friends unfortunately ended up in prison, passed away, or found themselves bound to a life of poverty doing manual labor or odd jobs. Making it out of this grim situation while others stayed behind, remaining systemically poor and disadvantaged, went on to haunt me later in life. I suffered from "survivor's guilt," the shame associated with being spared from a tragedy while others continue to suffer.

My parents grew up in the heart of London in an area known as Leytonstone. Like the rest of the East End, Leytonstone took the brunt of Hitler's World War II Luftwaffe blitz bombing raids in the early 1940s. The tough, hardworking population pulled together, living through blackouts, food rations, and nights spent in corrugated metal garden shelters known as Anderson shelters or indoors under specially constructed kitchen tables known as Morrison shelters. I remember my grandfather telling me stories about removing metal park fences near Epping Forest in London and loading them into a military truck so they could be melted down and reused for the war effort.

The people who lived through the war emerged much more resilient and resourceful. The physical scars from that time are still visible today; unfilled bomb craters scatter the city and serve as a reminder of past atrocities. The emotional scars went on to shape future generations, who valued work ethic and didn't take small things for granted. Food rationing was still in place after the war, and nothing went to waste. Each time our family's communal bar of soap used for bathing became too small to function, we saved it in a plastic container with a lid that screwed down to compress it. A handful of discarded soap bars saved this way became a new, family-sized bar of soap.

My parent's lives intersected a couple of times while they were growing up in Leytonstone. They worked together at a local supermarket on weekends, and they were both members of their school's performing arts program—my mother a singer, my father a lighting technician. A romance blossomed and they soon became inseparable. They started dating during a school opera production.

Eventually, they both got entry-level jobs in different departments at a large British bank.

When my sister was born, my parents decided that my mother would stay at home and take care of the children and my father would provide for the family financially. In my mother, I witnessed compassion, empathy, kindness, and a dedication to her children. Her sacrifices made it possible for my father to work long hours and build a career.

In my father, I witnessed a work ethic that would shape me forever. The formula seemed straightforward: get up, show up, work hard, and good things will happen. I watched him go to work before the sun came up and return home after dinner. He was recognized as a top performer in the bank and was offered a job in the main international office, located in the heart of London's financial district. I saw how hard other people's lives were around us, and I was grateful to have someone working to keep our family safe and sheltered.

My father's approach to work never wavered. He landed another promotion that temporarily relocated us to Ontario, Canada. It was a beautiful place. I had never seen snow before living there, and the people were friendly and kind. I have a lot of fond memories from that time, mostly involving winter activities like cross-country skiing and snowshoeing. We lived in Canada for just over two years before my father's next promotion and our rotation to the United States.

We moved to Dallas, Texas, where I fell in love with America. The sun was shining, the houses were huge and detached from the other houses, the roads were wide, the cars were spacious, people seemed relaxed and happy, and some of my friends even had swimming pools!

After a few years eating generously filled plates of Texas barbecue, playing on a Little League team, and going to rodeos, my father's rotation expired and we were forced to move back to London to the small home I grew up in. While we were away, a tenant had been leasing our house, and we came back to find it ransacked. The tenant had stolen everything, destroyed the house, and skipped out on rent payments; he even took the bulbs out of their sockets. We knew the tenant was serving a small stint in prison for an unrelated infraction, so we installed metal bars over the skylight in case he got out and wanted to revisit his old home. Overnight, I had gone from living in a wealthy Dallas suburb surrounded by friends and swimming pools to a small, trashed attached row home in London.

Standing in that house, assessing my new reality as I looked up at the gray sky through what looked like prison bars, my motivation was born. I was now and forever motivated to not be poor. My mother used to say that money doesn't buy happiness, but on that day, I learned that money does buy security, comfort, and freedom of movement.

I desperately wanted to move back to America. I didn't hate England. In fact, I loved the natural beauty of the countryside and was fascinated by its rich history, but I hated the way its society was structured and I missed the carefree atmosphere I experienced in the States.

England has a rigid and well-established class system that has been exported for centuries to colonies throughout the world; you need look no further than India's caste structure as an example. Essentially, the time, place, and bloodline into which you are born determine your class, which in turn limits or expands your job prospects and ability to accumulate wealth.

The southeastern part of England, near London, was crowded; the rates of unemployment, crime, and domestic abuse were high; and people spoke with cockney accents. Just a few hours north, you could find sprawling estates, historical manors, and wealthy families who spoke the "Queen's English." The accumulation of wealth among a tiny fraction of the population is not unique to England, but the ability to break out of your predetermined class and into a better way of life without the right pedigree in England seemed totally unattainable to me.

When I turned twelve, our family was assigned another rotation in America. My father's hard work was paying off again—he earned another promotion at the bank, this time working in New York City! The bank put us up in a house located in an affluent New Jersey suburb close to a train station convenient for commuting to the city. We were back in America, and this time I had no plans of leaving. I didn't know how we would stay, but I knew that working hard, being uncomfortable, and showing up would lead to security, freedom, and comfort, so I got to work.

In middle school, I started a car-washing business. In the summer months, I went door to door with a bucket, some car soap, and a couple of towels. I knew how much the local car wash charged for a basic wash and vacuum, so I charged the same. In my opinion, I actually did a better job than the car wash because I took my time washing each car by hand and making sure it was sparkling before ringing the doorbell to show off my work.

Eventually, I realized that people would come to me, which meant I wouldn't have to borrow their hoses and vacuums or run home for dry towels. I set up a sign on our driveway advertising a car wash and vacuum for twenty dollars. We lived near a major highway, so I got a good amount of traffic as cars came off the exit ramp. I set up a lawn chair for my customers so they could relax while I worked. Business was booming and, for a thirteen-year-old, I was flush with cash.

I met all kinds of people on those summer days when the car wash sign was up. I remember one interesting gentleman who pulled up in a vintage Pontiac wearing a leather jacket. He tipped me with a pack of menthol cigarettes and cautioned me not to smoke them all at once. I talked with the customers, asking them where they were headed and what made them stop for a car wash. People seem tickled that this kid was washing cars and making small talk, and I enjoyed it. Acting like a grown-up and holding real conversations felt good.

In the winter months, I started a snow removal business. I printed some flimsy business cards on our dot matrix printer. On days when school was canceled due to snow, instead of joining most of my friends who were out sledding, I got up early to knock on doors and offer fast, friendly, reasonably priced snow removal services using my parents' shovel and some elbow grease. I had a lot of competition when that white gold started falling, so I had to do an extra good job to differentiate my services from the professional outfits. Eventually, I had regular customers who would turn away my competition and wait for me to clear the snow from their drives. I liked my customers and I wanted to do a good job for them, despite my lack of professional plowing equipment.

One older lady always invited me in for hot chocolate after I was done clearing her snow. I think she looked forward to snow days so she could have some company and conversation over a cup of cocoa. The professional guys probably would have done a better and faster job, but my customers wanted to work with somebody local and reliable whom they liked and trusted.

On one occasion, an older man who lived down the street called and asked if I could clear his drive quickly because an ambulance was coming to take his wife to the hospital. I called a nearby friend to come and help so we could get it done before the ambulance arrived. The man was thrilled that we cleared the snow so quickly. His wife was carried out on a stretcher across a clean driveway into the back of the waiting ambulance. (She was okay. She just needed oxygen.) I told the man I couldn't accept his money, but he insisted and gave us triple our normal rate.

One day my mother's friend's regular babysitter canceled at the last minute. She had dinner plans for the evening, so she urgently needed someone to babysit on very short notice. My mother asked if I would be interested and, of course, I said yes.

I discovered that hanging out with kids and making sure they were fed and safe was an easy way to make money. In order to secure more babysitting gigs, I became a Red Cross certified babysitter, which meant I was trained in CPR, choking protocols, inappropriate touching, and the basic principles of child psychology. I was added to the local certified babysitter list. Reliable babysitters were hard to find, and reliable babysitters certified by the Red Cross were even more scarce. As a result, I had a regular list of well-paying clients who filled my calendar with their child-free date nights.

During high school, I worked at a local animal hospital, doing anything that needed doing. I started cleaning up after the animals and eventually found my responsibilities expanding to assisting with surgeries, doing fecal assays under a microscope looking for parasites, and staying overnight monitoring critical patients. I worked all holidays, including Christmas, because the animals needed care and I got paid double time!

As I got a little older and stronger, I got a summer job as a golf caddy at the local country club. Golf caddies didn't get paid for showing up. Payment was rendered only after carrying two bags for eighteen holes, roughly four hours. You couldn't carry bags unless you were chosen by Dave, the caddy master, or you were specifically requested by a member.

Some days I would show up at the caddy shack early in the morning and wait eight hours without getting selected, which meant no pay that day. I didn't know it at the time, but Dave was testing me to see if I would stick with it and keep showing up. I never liked sitting idle, so on the days I waited around the caddy shack, I would ask Dave if there was anything I could do to help him out. He usually handed me a broom and told me to sweep up, which I gladly did. Eventually, Dave started choosing me to caddy early in the day, which was great because that meant I had time to work two rounds before it got dark, which doubled my take-home pay.

Being a golf caddy involved so much more than simply walking eighteen holes for four hours or thirty-six holes for eight hours. To be an excellent caddy, you had to start with the right club selection off the tee. Then you had to fore caddy (stand about a hundred yards down the fairway before the golfers drive so you can spot where their balls land), keep the clubs clean all day, read putting greens, call out distances, replace divots, and recommend clubs. You also had to learn and adhere to a lot of etiquette, like not standing in the golfer's peripheral vision during a swing, not stepping on the putting line, keeping the pin shadow out of the way, stopping the flag from flapping in the wind, raking bunkers, and so on. It was hard work and physically exhausting.

These country club members had money, and lots of it; they had to drop six figures just to be considered for membership at the exclusive club. Some members sincerely appreciated how hard I was working to ensure they had a pleasant day on the course; they rewarded me with lunch after the first nine holes and a generous tip at the end of the round. Some members wanted to engage in friendly conversation for the entire round and began requesting me by name.

Other members were unpleasant. They treated me like a servant, didn't offer lunch, and paid the bare minimum. I vividly remember on one occasion caddying for an older man who didn't say much. The man was not playing well, he hit a lot of balls into the woods, and he became grumpier and more frustrated as the day progressed. I hustled for him as I always did—the skill level of the golfers never affected my level of service. I exerted the same level of effort for professionals as I did for newbies. Nevertheless, as we approached the eighteenth hole, the man turned to me and began blaming me for his poor performance. "You lost my ball back on seven and misread the green on twelve." He waited until the eighteenth hole to tell me how poorly I did in order to justify the lack of tip that awaited me at the end of that hole.

The lessons I learned on those links stuck with me forever. First, I always tip service workers generously, and second, having money doesn't entitle you to act like an asshole.

One summer, my parents bought me an expensive camera as a gift. I felt guilty that they spent so much money, so I looked for ways to use the camera to generate income. I decided to start an online photography business. I set up a website and took pictures of historic buildings in town. I framed them, created custom mats, and offered them for sale to the building owners for a healthy profit. Building owners usually had lots of money and were eager to memorialize their real estate acquisitions.

My photographic services were not limited to buildings. Our town had a parade every year on the Fourth of July. I took pictures of the people in the parade, found out where they lived (their names were usually on a banner or on the side of the cars), and mailed them proofs of the pictures available for purchase. Who doesn't want a picture of themselves in a parade? People dropped off cash and checks at my parents' house in exchange for a CD of royalty-free digital images. I had a couple of pricing packages available; they could purchase only their photos or, for a little more money, all of the parade photos.

It was clear to me that America was the land of opportunity for those willing to put in the work. The only limit was my imagination. But not everything in America was sunshine and roses. One of my high school English teachers was a nasty man. He was angry, argumentative, and generally not a nice person. He hated me. I'm not sure what I did to deserve his attention, but often I was the focus of his ire. He was the archetypal bad teacher, the "You will never amount to anything!" kind of guy.

This teacher once returned an assignment to me covered in red ink. The assignment was to write poems using a variety of metrics, like iambic pentameter. I had written a poem about my desire to own a luxury British car, specifically a Bentley. He wrote in the margin, "Why and when would you be in a Bentley! Logic?" I'm not sure what he meant, but I interpreted his comment as a person like me would never be able to afford a car like that, and I was motivated to prove him wrong. I didn't necessarily expect to literally purchase a Bentley one day, but I wasn't going to let this guy set limits on my potential. Who was he to say what kind of car I should be driving? I kept that assignment (Fig. 1) and looked at it throughout my career as a reminder that some people don't believe in me and are actively betting against me. I'm grateful for those people; nothing motivates me more than a nonbeliever.

After high school, we stayed in America and became citizens of the United States. My sister was the first member of our family to graduate from a four-year college, and I followed her shortly after.

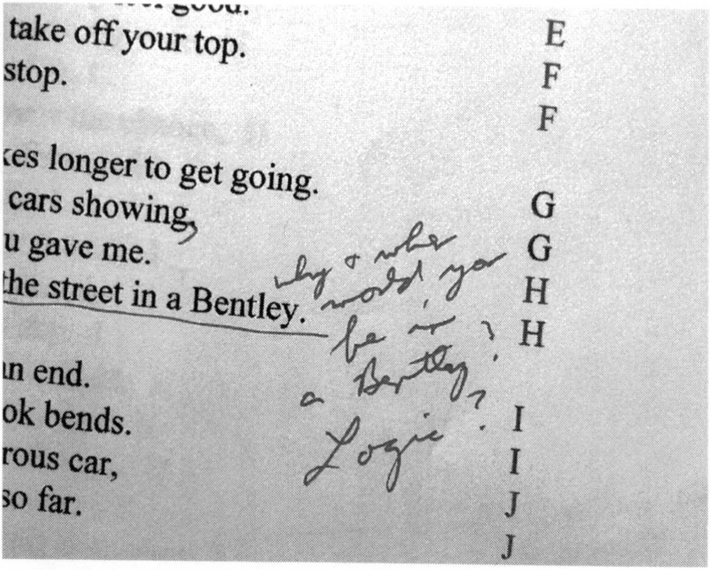
take off your top. E
stop. F
F
kes longer to get going.
cars showing, G
u gave me. G
the street in a Bentley. H
H
n end.
ok bends. I
rous car, I
so far. J
J

Fig. 1. My English assignment: "Why & when would you be in a Bentley! Logic?"

> Throughout your career, people will try to stifle your progress and limit your potential by doubting your vision and questioning your ability. Use their negativity as fuel to achieve great things. You don't need permission or consent from anybody to achieve greatness; silently work toward your goal and emerge triumphantly. When you set audacious visions, you can achieve your wildest dreams. Keep raising the bar and proving them wrong!

While in college, I got an unpaid internship at a major financial services firm in the evenings. In the mornings, I worked in the campus dining hall prepping huge quantities of food and washing hundreds of dishes. Working in that dining hall was one of the most enjoyable jobs I ever had. A majority of my morning-shift coworkers were ex-convicts, and they were some of the best, salt-of-the-earth, funniest people I have ever met. If you haven't danced to Mystikal's "Shake Ya Ass" at seven in the morning, you haven't lived. And to this day, I can make a giant bowl of salad for a hundred people in under two minutes.

I worked those jobs along with a few other gigs while taking an extra heavy course load and graduating a full semester early. My guidance counselors were concerned that I was trying to tackle too much and called me a workaholic. I respectfully disagreed with their assessment. I believed that most students had plenty of free time; they just squandered it. If they were to wake up earlier and spend less time in bars, they could achieve a lot more. Don't get me wrong. I had fun in college (and drank too much), but my main goal was to get out into the real world and start a career of my own.

Clearly, the root of my motivation was focused on not being poor, but I also was driven by survivor's guilt. I felt that I shouldn't squander any opportunity that I was fortunate enough to encounter. But why sales and why leadership?

Sales is an unusual profession. It's like running your own business but with less risk and overhead. As a sales rep, you experience a direct correlation between your effort and your results. Perhaps most importantly, your earning potential is usually bound only by how much you can sell. A career in sales was far from my first choice but, ultimately, it was the only profession I believed would provide unlimited fuel to feed my motivation.

After graduating from college, I was expecting a river of job opportunities to appear before me, but that did not happen. The cold reality was that despite all of my hard work and hustle, I had accomplished nothing of substance and the world owed me nothing. I rented a cheap, one-bedroom garden apartment near my old college campus, because I was familiar with the area and it was all I could afford with the little savings I had accumulated from my part-time jobs. I printed some résumés and walked into random office buildings, asking if they were hiring. I filled out a lot of applications and rarely heard back.

I eventually landed an interview with a small Boston-based tech company that had a branch office in New Jersey. I told the hiring manager, Lou, that I had no experience and the only thing I could offer him was my work ethic and my time. I asked Lou if I could work for one week on a trial basis with no pay because I was confident that he would be impressed. My strategy must have worked because Lou hired me on the spot. I landed my first real job as a sales rep for an Information Technology (IT) Value Added Reseller (VAR).

The role of an IT VAR is to align customers' needs with manufacturers' products, add some complementary and high-margin services, drop-ship the equipment directly to the customer, take a profit, and repeat. I applied everything I had learned over the years to my new job as a sales rep. I went door to door handing out letters and business cards (just like my snow clearing days), asking for meetings. I made calls, sent emails, hosted seminars, met manufacturers, and showed up anywhere I was invited—and some places I wasn't.

Lou was a great sales leader. He treated his team like a family and assembled a group of like-minded, hardworking individuals. I actually looked forward to going to work every day. Lou took me under his wing. He gave me his old suits to wear before I could afford my own, he was there when I needed advice, he fought on my behalf, and he gave me tough feedback to help me improve. I am forever grateful for Lou's leadership; it became the foundation upon which I developed my own leadership style and philosophy.

After almost four years working with Lou, I was recruited by Mike, a sales leader at one of the largest manufacturers we represented. This manufacturer was (and still is) one of the largest high-tech manufacturers in the world. It was there I spent almost a decade becoming a sales leader.

ANALYSIS

My personal journey of self-reflection was eye opening. By being brutally honest with myself, I drew a lot of conclusions.

I moved around a lot as a kid. Every time I established close friendships, we moved to a new country and I would have to say goodbye. I must have learned at a young age that the way to avoid the pain of saying goodbye to dear friends was to be a loner and not allow people to get too close. People later viewed that behavior as standoffish or unapproachable, but it was really a defense mechanism to avoid the pain of losing a friend.

Being exposed to two worlds was another formative experience. In one instant I was part of a seemingly middle-class American family with boundless opportunities, and in the next I was a lower-class Londoner with limited prospects. I lacked a sense of identity and felt a lack of control. This explains why I now crave control in every aspect of my life and have to remind myself to relinquish it at times.

Moving around forced me to adapt, pivot, and assimilate to wildly different cultures and styles of communication.

Washing cars for random strangers forced me to be comfortable speaking to anybody. These experiences provided me with valuable communication lessons, which I will share in greater detail in Chapter 10.

I also learned important lessons about sales and leadership during my formative years. My snow clearing customers were willing to pay more for my services even though a professional would have done a faster and better job. I learned that customers see value in relationships and appreciate a familiar and friendly face.

I'm sure a psychologist would draw their own conclusions from my experiences—fear, insecurity, self-esteem, ego, and so on—but I'll save those weightier topics for the therapist's couch.

Now that you've seen the level of self-examination I conducted to truly understand what shaped my personality, approach, demeanor, and motivation, I encourage you to spend some time embarking on your own introspection journey. Take the time and effort to find your "why." Block a couple of hours on your calendar, find a quiet room, think of your earliest childhood memory, and go from there. What sticks in your mind? What are you proud of? What do you regret? What trauma did you experience? Who was the greatest leader you worked with? Who was the worst leader? What did you learn from your early jobs and careers? Dig deep and don't be afraid to uncover wounds from the past. It's time to get to know who you really are. I'm confident you'll like who you find.

THREE

BECOMING A SALES LEADER

*A*ll leaders have an origin story, that moment they find themselves leading a group for the first time. For many people, that first leadership experience ignites a spark that breeds a lifelong passion. For others, that first moment is equally defining by cementing a loathing for the burdensome responsibility of leadership.

My earliest memory of leading a team was as a ten-year-old Boy Scout. I had the responsibility of being a "sixer," the leader of a group of six scouts who would lead the group through a week of camp away from home. The sixers were elected by the group and were responsible for all aspects of the team while at camp (adhering to rules, arriving on time, delegating tasks, competing in events, and so on). We were awarded points each day and assigned a score. At the end of the week, the pack with the most points won the Best Six Of Camp award (Fig. 2).

Every day, I reviewed with my team our point tally and current standing and let them know what we needed to do to earn more points and stay in the top position. The group was excited to win. We worked together every day to secure our position as the "best six at camp."

Fig. 2. My Best Six Of Camp award.

I remember on the last morning of camp, my group was showered, dressed, packed, and sitting silently in the dining hall waiting for the rest of the scouts to arrive. We looked like little soldiers; it felt good to be part of a well-oiled machine. We did end up winning, and my group was proud of what we had accomplished together. In that moment, I understood that we could achieve more as a team than as individuals, and I felt genuine joy in helping others push beyond their limits and experience the feeling of shared success.

Before I was a sixer, I was a Boy Scout. Before you can lead, you must follow. You can't lead a team unless you have walked a mile in their shoes. A team won't respect a leader who hasn't experienced the plight of the individual.

Can you imagine an Army cadet at boot camp taking orders from a drill sergeant who has never served in the military? It wouldn't happen because the US Army recognizes the importance of field experience prior to leadership. The Army has a well-established leadership and pay-grade ranking system starting with E-1 (Enlisted - pay grade 1) and going up to E-9 (sergeant major). The higher you advance, the more authority and responsibility you possess. Drill sergeants in the US Army are required to be a rank of E-5 through E-7, which means you must first serve as Corporal E-4.

Great sales organizations have employed similar principles as the US Army to ensure their leaders possess the necessary experience and qualifications to advance their teams.
Think of great sales leaders from your own career. More
than likely they have worked their way up through the ranks,
were humbled and enlightened by their experience, and
approached their teams with an appropriate mix of confidence and humility. Experience allows leaders to have genuine empathy for the plight of their teams and to offer credible
guidance and direction based on their shared experiences.

You might hear grumblings from sales teams that their
leaders have never "carried a bag," a phrase that dates
back to the days when door-to-door salespeople literally
carried a bag containing their products or samples for sale.
What the sales teams are really saying is, "Why should I listen to or respect this person who has never walked a mile
in my shoes?"

Before embarking on a sales leadership journey and
accepting a leadership role, you should have an established track record of success as a sales rep in some capacity
(Fig. 3). You will never earn the credibility nor the respect
of your team if you haven't lived through and conquered
the challenges they face every day.

A typical organization has a multitude of individual sales
roles. This chart shows what typical sales roles might look

like in order of seniority. Interesting to note is that some sales reps are considered leaders and have direct reports.

TITLE	DESCRIPTION
Business Development Rep	Entry-level role, responsible for fielding inbound requests and some level of outbound demand generation.
Inside Sales Rep	Responsible for outbound calling, hunting for new prospects, and supporting the outside sales reps.
Associate Sales Rep	Responsible for managing a small group of accounts or geography, typically with a low quota. May be paired with a more senior rep.
Outside Sales Rep	Solely responsible for delivering a quota in an assigned territory. Responsible for all aspects of sales (activity, pipeline, bookings, etc.).
Enterprise/ Strategic Sales Rep	A seasoned professional experienced with diverse account types, this person is responsible for some of the firm's largest and most lucrative accounts and prospects and understands how to structure and run long-term strategic sales pursuits.
Large/Key Account Manager	This person may only have a couple of accounts but has significant revenue responsibility in a higher touch environment with all the attributes of an enterprise or strategic sales rep.
Global Account Manager (GAM)	The global account manager (GAM) typically has global responsibility for a single or a few large customer(s). Usually the GAM will be a formal leader with direct reports such as product specialists, local account managers, etc.
Client Director/ Exectutive Sponsor	The highest rank for an individual seller is client director or executive sponsor. This person is considered an executive, will usually have direct reports, and is ultimately resposible for all revenue and growth within a specific account.

Fig. 3. Typical sales roles.

The ultimate role of the sales leader is to help sales reps sell—it's that simple. The best way for sales leaders to help reps sell is to share lessons and guidance from their own experiences, remove obstacles, and coach the reps toward successful outcomes.

Assuming you have demonstrated success in your role as a sales rep and you've conducted a thorough self-examination to uncover your "why," then you probably are starting to establish a leadership philosophy. Once you feel ready to secure a formal leadership role, the next step is to make your intentions known.

At this point you have met the unwritten prerequisites of formal leadership and have determined that you are ready for a leadership role, but unfortunately you might be the only person who knows this. When that next leadership role opens, you want to be the uncontested person everyone is already thinking of as the natural successor. Most people wait around for spots to open before they throw their hats in the ring, only to take everyone by surprise by "coming out of nowhere." Nobody likes surprises, especially when it comes to making important hiring and promotion decisions. I can almost guarantee your manager already has a short list of high-potential leadership successors for that role you think should be yours. Every leader has a succession plan and a talent bench. If you aren't sure whether or not you are part of that plan, you aren't.

As a sales rep looking to transition into leadership, plan to embark on a six- to twelve-month brand-building journey prior to going for a leadership role. That way, when the role becomes available, you are the uncontested choice. Inform your immediate manager now that you aspire to embark on a formal leadership journey and ask for support. Tell your manager that you are not ready today (even if you believe you are) but you are prepared to take all the necessary steps prior to the next leadership opportunity opening. Show self-awareness and humility and give your manager the opportunity to disagree.

Then, as preparation for the leadership role, demonstrate leadership in your current role without the title. Your team needs to consider you a leader, and at least ten people outside of your direct team should also consider you a leader.

I've conducted countless interviews with people for leadership positions who were sure they were getting the job and were devastated when they didn't. I always offer feedback and advice to people who didn't get the job, and the conversation usually goes the same way every time:

Me: Find ways to be a leader today, without the title.
Everything you just laid out in your leadership plan

sounds great, but you aren't doing any of it today.
Why?

Candidate: I'm not doing it because I don't have the job
yet and I'm not the leader.

Me: Don't wait to be in the job to do the job. You can
start today.

A sales rep can be a team leader in so many ways, but
most sales reps are so focused on themselves that even
their motivations for getting into leadership are selfish:
ego, title, pay, and recognition.

Somebody once told me, do what your manager does
and you will become a manager. Put simply, if you want
to become a leader, demonstrate leadership. Here are ten
specific ways you can demonstrate leadership immediately
as a sales rep without a leadership title, thereby bolstering
your brand as a leader and becoming a viable and uncontested leadership candidate:

1. **Show your expertise.** Ask your manager if you can
   share a best practice or speak on a topic with the
   team during your next team meeting.

2. **Embrace altruism.** Host a charitable fundraising
   event for a cause you truly care about. Invite

coworkers to participate and help raise funds outside of work. Show your altruistic side and leverage your platform.

3. **Encourage team interaction.** Host a weekly call for your peers to share competitive insights, market trends, objection handling, product updates, and the like.

4. **Interview and recruit talent.** Pass résumés to your manager, screen candidates, and refer people to HR. Ultimately, you are looking for the person who will replace you.

5. **Have a business plan.** You don't need to be a leader to have a plan for the team. Show your leaders that you have put thought into the future of your team and the company. What are some things you could do to help move the needle today and drive revenue?

6. **Be selfless.** Great leaders put their team, the company, and everything else before their own interests. Find ways to help people and ask for nothing in return. Do things for the good of the

company, not for the good of your wallet. If your neighbor works at a company that your peer is trying to sell to, make the introduction and don't ask for a share of the revenue. Do it because it's the right thing to do for the company and you want your peer to be successful. If you see people on your team struggling, take them under your wing and offer them coaching, mentoring, and guidance.

7. **Show up!** It sounds easy but most people don't do it. Try showing up to everything for an entire month. Accept every invite and say yes to everything that crosses your desk. Dinners, events, meetings, golf outings, networking groups...it will be exhausting, but great things *always* happen when you show up. If people don't see you, they aren't thinking about you.

8. **Ask for feedback.** Not only is soliciting feedback a great way to uncover blind spots, the mere act of asking for feedback demonstrates a willingness to improve and shows that you want to understand your brand and take control of it. Great leaders never stop learning; they are always looking for ways to improve.

9. **Be positive.** People want to be around people
    that make them feel good. Smile a lot. Focus on
    the positives in conversations. Don't engage in
    gossip or talk behind people's backs. If you don't
    have anything positive to say about someone, it's
    better left unsaid—unless the person is negatively
    impacting your business or you have witnessed
    something unethical. In that case, address it
    honestly with the offender directly or even with
    Human Resources.

10. **Carry yourself with confidence.** Body language is
    so important in every aspect of our lives. The way
    you carry yourself sends a message before you even
    open your mouth. Imagine you are about to walk
    into a meeting that you are not looking forward
    to. Maybe you are about to come face-to-face with
    an angry client who has issues with your product.
    As you walk into the meeting room, your spouse
    calls to tell you that you just won the lottery! It's a
    life-changing sum of money and you never have to
    work again! Your body language would instantly
    change—your shoulders would relax and roll back,
    your chest would push out, your head would lift,
    your throat would relax, and you would feel calm

and confident. You probably wouldn't care about what anyone thinks, and the meeting suddenly would seem less important. Try to capture that feeling before every interaction. It's contagious. It sends a strong message of positivity and calm, which people often describe as "executive presence." They are drawn to it and want more of it.

Assuming you've done all the hard work to get to the point where you are considered the uncontested choice for the next leadership role that opens, the only thing standing in your way now is the interview process.

FOUR

INTERVIEW LIKE
A LEADER

The interview process can be frustrating and unpredictable. Most companies have too many interviewees for a single position, the process usually takes too long, insufficient (or no) feedback is provided, the interviewers ask trick questions, and they are not trained properly so they ask inappropriate or illegal questions. You will encounter a wide variety of interview approaches throughout your career. Some larger organizations use a bank of predetermined questions designed to target certain areas of your personality, such as "Tell me about a time you failed. What happened and why?" or "Tell me about a time you disagreed with your manager." Some companies want you to role-play, and others will stress test you by creating a combative atmosphere to see how you react under pressure. All these variables are outside of your control, but you do have full control over your words and actions.

I once worked at a large company where I was surrounded by some really strong, talented individuals. Every year, we all competed for one or two open job promotions. We referred to it as the "logjam," meaning we had a lot of strong talent but only a few jobs available. I knew that if I was going to have a legitimate shot against these people, I was going to have to really differentiate myself, so I searched for help.

A friend referred me to a career coach—let's call him Tom. Tom had a passion for helping people to elevate their brands and take charge of their careers. He was highly sought after and charged a premium for his services. I paid him in cash and we met in my office after work, where he conducted mock interviews with me. I answered his questions standing up, sitting down, with a presentation, without a presentation, with objections, without objections, and so on. We practiced every scenario he could think of.

Tom's strategy was to get me comfortable with a variety of situations, because you have no control over the way an interview is conducted or the questions asked. In fact, in some interviews, no questions will be asked; instead you will be given an hour to sell yourself, present a business plan, or simply talk. Not knowing what to expect can leave you feeling unprepared, insecure, and unconfident—not good feelings to have before an interview. What if there was a way to know that you can handle anything that comes your way? What if you had an anecdote and a real-world example prepared for any question asked of you? It would be like having all the answers to a test and would provide some much-needed confidence.

Some people "interview well" because they've figured out the formula. Fortunately, you can be one of those people. I have successfully used a proven interview preparation method for years, and it is fairly easy to adopt. Here's how it works.

Step 1: Know Your Story and Be Able to Articulate It In Two Minutes or Less

If somebody says, "Tell me about yourself," you should feel very comfortable telling your story. My answer to that question is a two-minute timeline that touches on my track record, my motivations, a couple of personal elements to show my human side, and some commentary about my direction and aspirations and why this is the right role for me at the right company at the right time. I also sprinkle in a little self-deprecation, which is a very powerful tool if you need to win somebody over in a short period of time. I will say something like, "I feel fortunate just to be in the running. I could have just as easily found myself delivering pizzas." It seems counterintuitive to downplay your abilities during an interview, but I promise you that telling someone how amazing you are is never well received. People will always hire somebody humble, likable, modest, and coachable over somebody who is arrogant or narcissistic, even if the latter is more qualified.

Step 2: Prepare Three Mental Buckets that You Can Tie Interview Questions Back To

My career coach, Tom, taught me that this is one of the most important things you can do before an interview. A "mental bucket" is a focus area. For a leadership role, your three mental buckets might be Track Record, Leadership, and Business Plan. Most interview questions will fall into one of these categories. A question might not always fit *perfectly*, but with a little finesse, you can tie any question into one of your buckets and have confidence in knowing what you are about to say. For each mental bucket, prepare an anecdote, a real-life example, an opinion, and references. For example, in my Leadership bucket, I have a short story about a great leader I have worked with, and

I have a real-world example of a way in which I have demonstrated similar leadership. I have a strong opinion about what it takes to be a great leader (humility, empathy, growth mindset, bias for action, etc.) and am prepared to discuss my leadership philosophy. In this way, during an interview I can answer any question related to leadership with information "pulled" from my Leadership bucket. If you do nothing else, study your three buckets, memorize your answers, and walk into the interview with confidence!

Step 3: **Ask Questions and Listen More Than You Speak**

An interview is usually a dialogue, not a one-sided barrage of questions. The people conducting the interview are in positions of power and are in the interviewer role for a reason. They likely have a lot of experience and perhaps have even been in a role like the one you are interviewing for. Ask them about their journey, their stories, and how they got to where they are. Ask them what they like and dislike about the company. Ask them what else you should be doing and what they would do if they were in your shoes. Asking questions in an interview serves two purposes. First, people enjoy talking about themselves, and second, it shows that you don't have all the answers and are willing to listen, learn, and solicit input from others, which are all attributes of great leaders.

Step 4: **Have an Opinion and Have a Plan**

Demonstrating that you have put thought and time into solving real issues associated with the role you are seeking is a critical and often overlooked part of any interview. Although you might not be asked for a plan, you should prepare one and have it professionally printed and bound. Ideally, for in-person interviews, send it to the interviewer the night before. If you really want to go the extra mile, deliver a hard copy via an overnight shipping service and include a handwritten note.

Your plan should be concise, it should leverage your three mental buckets as primary talking points, and, most importantly, it should be tailored to the specific role you are interviewing for. If you are seeking a people leadership role, you should have an opinion about the team, the people, and the specific issues they are facing. Admit that you don't have all the answers and that you will need to listen and learn before taking any action.

Keep in mind that you are being hired to perform a specific task, but ultimately you are being hired to make the lives of those above you easier. Having a plan shows you have taken an important step toward owning the team and all of its issues, problems, and challenges. When I'm interviewing leadership candidates who will report to me, I am

INTERVIEW LIKE A LEADER

not looking for someone who is going to dump more work on my plate—quite the opposite. I need someone who can take things off my plate, somebody who can act autonomously and make decisions appropriately without constant supervision or permission. A plan demonstrates that you are that type of candidate.

Your plan doesn't need to be perfect; in fact, it shouldn't be. But you should interview as if you are getting the job, and you need a plan to do the job. Waiting until you have the job to formulate a plan is akin to changing the tires on a moving car.

Part of your plan should include how you will be spending time in the first thirty days, sixty days, and ninety days (often called a 30-60-90). For the most part, your first thirty days should be spent in observation mode, meeting with the team, rolling up your sleeves, dismissing or confirming preconceived notions, and spending time in the field. Politicians call this time a "listening tour," but in reality, you are using this time to solidify your opinions and tighten up your plan. The first thirty days is a critical time as a new leader to set the tone, set clear expectations, and establish what type of leadership people can expect from you.

People often fall into the trap of trying to immediately be liked by the team and becoming everyone's best friend.

There is a secret to setting the appropriate tone in the first thirty days, and it's not natural or comfortable for most people: Come out of the gate strong. You can always soften up later, but starting weak and toughening up later is impossible. Think about the advice given to people headed to prison: "Come out swinging and show them you aren't to be messed with." If you show up crying your first night, you are going to have a rough time serving the rest of your sentence.

The first sixty days should be spent providing feedback, addressing problem areas, and course correcting. If you see a problem, fix the problem. You were hired for a reason and you need to trust your gut. The first sixty days is the perfect time to let people know what you observed in the first thirty days, why it's a problem, and how you are going to help them resolve it.

The first ninety days is when you take action. By now people know what to expect from you and are aware of areas that need improvement. You can't allow problems to fester; they will only get worse. Beyond ninety days, you can rate your own performance, assign yourself a grade, share it with your team, ask for their feedback, and let them know what you are working on to better serve as their leader moving forward.

INTERVIEW LIKE A LEADER

Step 5: **Close Them!**

This is such a simple step but so many people forget. Like we always tell our sales reps, ask for the business! Ask your interviewers how they think the interview went. Do they have any concerns? Are they comfortable endorsing you for the position? Is there anything they would like to dig deeper on? Do you have their support?

Step 6: **Follow Up**

Letter writing and following up is a lost art. You don't have to send a handwritten note, although it's a nice touch, but at the very least you should follow up with an email thanking the interviewers for their time, confirming next steps, and establishing your excitement to move forward in the process. Your follow-up communication should not be a generic form letter. It should reference specific details from your conversation, something like, "I really enjoyed our discussion about accelerating revenue during times of constrained supply chain." If you don't have the interviewers' email addresses, ask the recruiter to send your follow-up letter for you.

Interviews are fluid and inconsistent. Not everything will fit neatly into your three mental buckets, and some questions are designed to throw you off. When answering questions in a leadership interview, put yourself in the shoes of the shareholders or CEO and think in terms of what is best for the company. For example, a common interview question is "How would you feel if you don't get the job?" Most people react with a knee-jerk, visceral response. "I would be disappointed! I've worked hard for this and I think I'm the right person for the job!" This is not an effective answer. Put yourself in the shoes of the CEO; if you don't get the job, it means the interviewers have identified somebody they feel is better suited for the role and the company. Here's a better answer to that question: "Of course, I would be disappointed initially, but I want what is best for the team and the company. If I don't get this job, that means you have found somebody who is a better fit and that's a great thing for the company and, ultimately, for me."

Being a leader means you have to think like a leader at all times. Great leaders think of their teams, their companies, and a larger mission beyond their own selfish desires. I once told an interviewer that if I didn't get the job, I would be relieved because I knew how much effort it would take to do the job well. If somebody else was better suited for the role and willing to put in the hard work required, that would be a great thing—they should hire that person immediately! I got that job.

Another trap people fall into during interviews is trying to have all the answers. I have stepped on this land mine myself many times. You might encounter a question about a specific issue or project that you have no idea about. Rather than trying to formulate an answer on the spot, say, "I have no idea, but I would figure it out" or "I'm not familiar with that. Please tell me more." Being vulnerable in an interview setting is a rare and refreshing scene. Great leaders don't know it all, and they are not expected to, but they should be willing to listen, learn, and solicit help from others.

When you get the job and it has been publicly and officially announced, the first people you should reach out to are the people who didn't get the job, especially if they are now going to report to you. Let them know you will do what you can to support them on their journeys and get them to where they want to be. Don't overpromise anything. They didn't get the job for a reason, which is why you should tell them only that you will do what you *can*. It's possible that they will never get into leadership; perhaps it's not the right path for them. Having somebody on your team who harbors resentment toward you or who could potentially undermine your leadership will become a toxic issue if not addressed early.

FIVE

FORTY SECRETS

There are no silver bullets that will make you a great sales leader, but there are some unspoken and sometimes unconscious secrets shared by the best leaders.

You know that confident, bright, and polished guy who gets up on stage in front of the whole company and effortlessly delivers a speech off the cuff? His secret is preparation.

He actually has crippling anxiety and detests public speaking; he was up all night practicing in front of a mirror and has rehearsed his speech a thousand times before getting near the stage. In fact, that same guy never speaks in front of a group unless he has memorized the first ten words that are going to come out of his mouth. Why? Because after the first ten confidently delivered words, you own the crowd and you are enjoying the moment.

Great leaders don't openly share their critical success factors for the same reason that magicians don't reveal their secrets. In this chapter, I share forty of the most important and impactful leadership secrets that you can implement immediately.

Book editors hate chapters like this. I know because they told me. A densely numbered list that throws off the overall chapter weighting is highly discouraged. However, I decided to keep this list intact rather than cutting it down or trying to unnaturally spread the advice throughout the book. I want to provide you with a single place to refer back to. I also want to provide an answer to the question, "If I only have time to read one chapter, which one should I read?" Here it is, forty secrets:

Secret 1: Always Listen More Than You Speak

You have two ears and one mouth; you should listen twice as much as you speak. There is a difference between listening and hearing. Most people are not great listeners. They might hear what you are saying, but they are thinking about their next meeting or formulating a response as they wait for their turn to talk. Being a generous listener is an attribute shared by great leaders, and it is something that you can practice every day.

The next time somebody talks to you (maybe your spouse or child), stop everything you are doing, look them in the eye, nod your head, and don't speak. Be totally in the moment with them. When they are finished talking, acknowledge and reinforce what you just heard using their same words, tone, and pace. Ask questions and demonstrate excitement. If this seems unnatural to you, you probably need more listening practice. Don't worry about those moments of awkward silence. People love to talk and will fill those gaps. In a world full of talkers, be a listener.

Secret 2: **Speak Plainly**

You might think that using large, obscure, hard-to-pronounce words or tech jargon is impressive and showcases your intelligence, but instead you are broadcasting your insecurity and will be perceived as unapproachable. I'm not suggesting that you dumb down your speech. Just use plain language and speak authentically and from the heart, like you would with a close family member or when having a beer with a friend.

Every year, new buzzwords and phrases crop up. A few years ago, everybody was "leaning in" and "leading from the front." People had become "thought leaders" and everything was getting "bifurcated." In a world where everybody is imitating everybody, you can be endearing and trusted simply by using tried and tested plain and simple language.

Secret 3: Be Vulnerable

Tell people your shortcomings. Share your fears and inse-curities. Show your human side and don't be afraid to appear weak—everyone is struggling with something. It takes a strong person to admit to having weaknesses. One of the greatest leaders I ever worked with had a habit of telling very personal stories and crying on stage. When I asked him about it, he said it wasn't a calculated move, but he was aware that if he could be vulnerable and authen-tic to the point of shedding actual tears, the entire group would feel comfortable doing the same. A team of authen-tic, vulnerable, humble people with shared struggles is a key element of a cohesive, high-functioning team.

Secret 4: Communicate Concisely

If you do nothing else, always search for opportunities to communicate complicated issues in a simple and concise manner. Think about one of the most complicated issues you have ever faced in the workplace. Now, explain that issue to your five-year-old nephew in four sentences or less—it's not easy, but it's possible.

Great leaders can articulate strong and difficult mes-sages using only a few words. We all have only 24 hours in a day; long emails won't get read, long speeches won't be absorbed, and action items will get lost. Find ways to reduce words and get straight to the point in all your communication. An ideal state of communication between leader and team exists when few to no words are required because you are operating under a high level of mutual trust and unified dedication toward achieving coauthored objectives.

Secret 5: **Act Like You Don't Care**

Remember that feeling we talked about earlier when your spouse called to tell you about winning the lottery? How your body language changed and nothing else seemed important? Capture that feeling and embrace it. People are generally stressed, anxious, and nervous all day. They are drawn to people who appear relaxed and carefree.

A less fun example than winning the lottery is confronting mortality. I once learned about the loss of a friend right before walking into a meeting. Suddenly, the meeting felt insignificant. My mind was elsewhere, and I really didn't care how the meeting went.

Sometimes the "I don't care" attitude comes from thinking you have no chance at winning and nothing to lose. I remember landing a big deal with a global manufacturer of plastic food wrap. I honestly didn't expect to win the deal because our price was higher and the customer didn't need all the features that our solution offered, but he ended up buying from me anyway. I asked the CIO why, and he said he loved that I "didn't seem to care if I got the deal or not." My competitor was apparently very pushy, and the customer felt like the other rep's next meal depended on this one sale. He figured if the rep was so desperate for the sale, then that must mean nobody is buying his product, so there must be an issue with it. Ultimately, I really *did* care, but I always tried to conceal that from my customer and, later in my leadership career, from my teams. There is a difference between passion and desperation.

The most eye-opening experience I had with "not caring" happened when I was working for a very large, multinational tech company. My senior vice president (let's call him Geoff) was in town from headquarters in California to spend time with the New York–based teams. Geoff seemed like a nice guy, but he was generally considered unapproachable. He had an intimidating air and was always in a rush. During his previous visits to New York, he was preoccupied with a group of eager executives fighting for a few minutes of his time, so I never spoke with him directly.

But this day was different. After almost a decade with the organization, I had accepted a new role at a different company and I was about to give my two weeks' notice. I was sitting in a conference room responding to emails when Geoff stopped in. He asked if he could join me as he needed to catch up on some work in a quiet place (without a gaggle of fawning executives). He asked how everything was going, and I told him everything was great. In fact, I told him I had never felt better. I was exercising more, I had cut alcohol out of my diet, I was sleeping better, and I was spending more quality time with my son.

Geoff looked up from his laptop and smiled. I could tell he wasn't expecting such a lengthy response. He said, "Man, I struggle with social drinking myself. There are so many events and dinners. How do you handle not drinking at those?" What followed was a normal, fun, relaxed interaction with a guy whom I barely spoke with in the past. To an outsider, we probably looked like old friends catching up and sharing a laugh. I was relaxed and authentic because I honestly didn't care what he thought. I was leaving the company, and I had nothing to lose. I felt comfortable, and I could tell my relaxed and confident nature put Geoff at ease as well.

People want to be around people who make them comfortable. I once worked with a marketing coordinator named Nathalie. If I was invited to an event, I always hoped Nathalie would be there. She was easy to talk to, introduced me to new people, and was generally fun to be around. If you struggle with acting like you don't care (because you really *do* care), try to be someone's Nathalie.

Put people at ease, try to relax, and don't take anything too seriously. A great leader once told me, "Twenty years from now, when we bump into each other on the beach, we won't remember all the business stuff, just the fun we had and the friends we made along the way."

Secret 6: Watch Your Grammar

Written communication is a critical component of successful leadership. Nothing will discredit you faster than a misused *their*, *there*, or *they're*. If you struggle in this department, hire an English tutor before it's *too* late.

Secret 7: Be Disciplined and Do What You Say You Are Going To Do

It sounds easy but so many leaders make commitments with no follow-through. If you tell people they won awards, actually send them the trophies. If you tell folks you will attend a dinner meeting, be there. Set an example by consistently doing what you say you are going to do.

Secret 8: Identify Your Moral Compass and a Concrete Set of Non-Negotiables

Too many leaders are willing to bend rules or violate ethics to drive results. That might pay off in the short term, but it only tarnishes your reputation in the long run. Never deviate from your moral code, even if it could cost you your job. All you have is your name and reputation. Communicate your moral code with your team and get commitment and buy-in that it will be adhered to. Better yet, ask your team for their input and coauthor a new team code of ethics. Coauthored plans are more likely to be embraced because people feel a sense of ownership.

Secret 9: **Be Visible**

You need to be out with your team, meeting customers, spending time in the field, and showing up. It's such a simple thing to do, but so many people take the easy path of hiding behind a laptop. You've probably heard idioms about showing up: belly up to the bar, sit in the chow hall, and—one of my favorites—you can't hunt from the lodge.

Being visible goes beyond just showing up in person. Find creative ways to promote your brand and extend your voice, things like creating a video message with a personal touch that gets distributed to your entire team. You can't physically be everywhere, but thanks to social media platforms and video tools, you can touch a lot of people at once. If you aren't in people's faces, you aren't on people's minds.

Secret 10: **Share Your Trust**

I once worked for a leader who was robotically professional. His words were carefully chosen, and he always held the corporate line. He could be described as a "cookie-cutter" corporate executive. It was only after about a year of working together that I saw a different side of him. We were in a conference room alone, watching somebody present on video. He muted our video system, looked at me, and said, "That guy sucks!" His comment was so out of character, I felt that he must really trust me to share his honest and unfiltered opinion, to show me an authentic side that most people don't get to see. He was a chameleon; he knew what to say and how to behave in different situations. He was just as comfortable on stage delivering a polished message as he was in a conference room with me sharing his disdain for the presenter. We went on to have a very strong working relationship built on a solid foundation of mutual trust.

In another instance, an executive leader told me in confidence that there was about to be a major organizational announcement. She wanted me to hear it directly from her first, before it became public. She provided insights into how the decisions were made and shared some of her personal thoughts on the matter. I felt like she was inviting me to peek behind the curtain and giving me a seat at the table.

Secret 11: **Enlist a Mentor**

It's hard to reach the summit of Everest without the support of sherpas and oxygen; the higher you climb, the more help you need. The same is true about leadership: you can't do this alone. Every great leader I've ever met has a mentor. A mentor is somebody who can guide you, provide you with tough feedback, and help you identify blind spots that might be hindering progress on your leadership journey. A mentor can help you evaluate a situation with a fresh set of eyes and an outside perspective. The time you spend with your mentor should not create any additional work for the mentor. You should come prepared with questions, issues you are dealing with, and topics of focus. Mentors will drop you pretty quickly if you are waiting for them to create an agenda or come up with topics for discussion. Also, mentor sessions should have an end date. Nobody wants to sign up as a perpetual mentor with no end in sight. I suggest starting with a monthly cadence for six months with a mutual option to renew—or not—in month seven.

Secret 12: **Promote Yourself**

Too often I see leaders doing great things in a vacuum because they don't want to self-aggrandize, brag about their accomplishments, or upstage their team members.

Being a great leader doesn't mean you should surrender all of your work and allow others to take credit. Broadcast the accomplishments of others, but also be proud of your own accomplishments. If you are doing great work and nobody knows about it, you are really doing a disservice to your peers and company by not sharing best practices. You can appropriately promote yourself in a variety of ways; it's okay to take credit for your work. Share a best practice with a larger audience outside of your team, host an all-hands meeting, and ask others to provide their endorsements.

Secret 13: **Choose and Memorize a Mantra**

A good mantra provides you with direction in challenging times. When I feel overwhelmed and all else fails, I go back to my mantra of ARC: Accountability, Recognition, and Consistency. I know that if I focus on only these three areas and nothing else, my team will be better off, and I will regain a sense of control.

Secret 14: **Employ a Battle Cry**

Kevin was one of the best sales leaders I ever worked for. He ended every email with three letters, EFD. Everybody at the company knew what it meant because he also ended every call and every presentation with the same letters.

More importantly, it was a phrase that unified because it was an internal code; you had to be part of his team to get it (which is why I won't share its meaning here). EFD was Kevin's battle cry. Just like General Custer commanding his men to "Charge!" at the Battle of Little Big Horn, when Kevin raised his fist in the air and screamed "EFD!", we all enthusiastically followed him into battle.

Secret 15: Be a Model Citizen

Look at the highest-ranking officers in your company. They probably don't drink too much at work events, they probably don't spout divisive political stances, and they probably don't tell off-color jokes or use foul language (except as an authenticity tool for sharing trust, as discussed in Secret 10). These people got to where they are for a reason, and it's a good idea to emulate their conduct.

Secret 16: Be Authentic

We all have a work version of ourselves that we present to coworkers so they see us in the best possible light, but we also all have a grittier home version of ourselves that is more relaxed and "real."

Bringing elements of your home version to work will be appreciated by your team. People can tell when you are not being authentic. It takes a great leader to speak authentically and genuinely to the team. Authenticity breeds trust, and trust is a key element to gaining followership.

Secret 17: **Focus On the Vital Few**

Focusing on doing a few things well is better than doing many things poorly. Imagine you were just elected Mayor of New York City. You might have run a campaign with an ambitious agenda, but you can't solve every problem the city faces during your short term in office, so you need to dedicate your time, energy, and resources to doing a few things and doing them well. Perhaps your first year in office you will assemble a task force to address the issue of homelessness. Perhaps the second year you will focus on infrastructure and repairing subway lines.

You need to choose what is important, clearly articulate your priorities, and help remove any distractions or noise that will deviate you from your vital few. As a sales leader, you are like an airplane pilot: you have only so many dials that you can tweak to get your plane to cruising altitude. Choose your dials wisely. If you choose the wrong one, pivot fast and move on or the plane could crash.

Choosing to focus on doing one thing effectively still requires a hundred other things. Let's say you decide you want to focus only on upgrading low-performing sales reps. To do so effectively, you need enablement, inspection,

field time, shadowing, mentoring, performance management, bench building, coaching, hiring, legal engagement,
human resources support, recognition, and much more.
Obviously, doing that "one thing" well requires a lot of
focus and dedication.

Secret 18: Smile

It sounds simple, yet deliberately choosing to be upbeat
and smiling is a game changer. It's important that you set
the weather for your team. Put another way, one of the
functions you serve as a leader is to be the thermostat, not
the thermometer, for your team. Think about air travel.
When you experience turbulence on a flight, you look to
the flight attendants for reassurance; if they are smiling
and confident, you will be too. For some people, smiling
comes naturally. But if you don't feel like smiling, think of
something that makes you happy: kids, family, vacation,
or even that martini you will have at the bar in a few hours.

Secret 19: Remember Dates and Details

Knowing the name of your employees' spouses or kids, the
breeds of their dogs, or their favorite basketball teams goes
a long way in showing them that you care and that they
are important. Gestures like sending a brief birthday or
anniversary note to a team member is what separates great

leaders from remarkable leaders. Some leaders focus only on this category and are ineffective in all other areas. You know that guy who sends you a message on your birthday every year and asks about your kids by name? You can't pinpoint exactly what he does and how he adds value to your organization, but he sticks around because he's likable and seems to care. Unfortunately, that guy is ineffective, both as an employee and as a leader. Remembering dates and details is important but does not stand on its own.

Secret 20: **Manage Up**

It's become trite corporate jargon, but all great leaders "manage up" extremely well. Managing up describes the way you interact with those higher up in your organization, doing whatever you can to help them do their jobs. The opposite, of course, is managing down, or interacting with subordinates. You can't effectively manage down until you have mastered managing up.

In simple terms, if you are managing up well, your immediate manager feels that you make life easier. Your manager trusts you to make effective decisions aligned with the company's goals, strategy, and vision.

The reward for effectively managing up is empowerment. Once you are empowered, you can shift your focus to your team, managing down and leading. If your team sees you struggling with or being undermined by your manager, they will lose all faith in your ability to execute and will ultimately go around you. A lot of people operate in a constant state of fear and anxiety, thinking, "I better do this or I could lose my job." You can't manage up effectively if you are operating in such a manner.

Imagine you are leading a team of salespeople. You have one rep (let's call him Bob) who copies you on every email, asks permission before doing anything, seems generally high strung, and constantly looks for validation. Now imagine another rep (let's call her Kathy) who has a quiet confidence, makes sound decisions, and almost seems slightly irritated when you call her for an update. Kathy runs her own business, she views you as an investor rather than a manager, she is confident in her own abilities, and she doesn't need your validation. Kathy doesn't need much from you, but when she does need something, she lets you know.

Kathy is managing up very well because she has earned your respect. You appreciate her strong work ethic and that she takes things off your plate and generally makes your life easier. Bob, on the other hand, seems unsure of himself. You assume he either isn't doing the right things and is nervous that you will find out, or he doesn't view himself as a valuable asset who provides a premium service. Of course, you would rather be like Kathy in your manager's eyes, but most people fall into the Bob category.

When you go to the car wash, usually you will see at least three levels of service available. The basic level might be an exterior wash, the next level up might include a carpet vacuum, and the premium option might include everything offered by the lesser options plus additional services like a tire shine and wax. All options result in your car getting washed, but the premium option is nice to have. Kathy knows she is providing you with a premium service and you are fortunate to have her on your team. Be like Kathy and only offer the premium service to those above you.

Secret 21: Don't Be a Jellyfish

The first time I heard this phrase, I struggled to wrap my head around it, but the concept is simple: own your decisions, stand behind them, and don't blame others. A peer once reached out to me when he was preparing to terminate an employee who had ongoing issues with performance. He wanted advice on talking points, and so I asked him to role-play with me as if I were the employee. He nervously cleared his throat and said, "As you know, our head of sales is looking at everyone's performance and your attainment is not up to the level he expects, and unfortunately he has asked me to let you go." Essentially this manager was telling his employee, "Sorry, this wasn't my decision. I'm just the messenger." He took this approach because the reality of the situation was uncomfortable and difficult to communicate. However, this is a weak tactic, like a jellyfish who drifts with the current. What he really wanted to say was, "I don't want you on my team. You are not doing what it takes to be successful. We've had this conversation multiple times, but your calendar is empty and I don't believe you have what it takes to make it here."

Communicating difficult news is not easy, but as a leader you have to own your decisions and communicate them clearly. The language I ultimately suggested my peer use in the conversation was, "As we've discussed, your performance has not been up to the level expected nor required to maintain your position at the company. We have tried to turn things around for a while, but we still are not seeing satisfactory results. At this point, I have made the decision to let you go. This decision is my own, it is final, and not open to further discussion."

This statement seems cold and heartless, but the truth is, the employee had been on notice for over a year and was essentially collecting a paycheck with almost zero effort exerted to turn things around. My peer did not owe his employee an apology—she created the situation herself—but he did owe her crystal clear and decisive communication. This strong approach left no room for debate or discussion, the employee was not surprised, she understood the decision, and the manager learned an important lesson. Own your decisions, especially the hard ones, and don't be a jellyfish.

Secret 22: **Keep a To-Do List**

Great leaders are sought-after individuals, which is reflected in their busy calendars; yet somehow, they never let anything fall through the cracks. Most of the great leaders I've spoken with maintain a perpetual to-do list. Imagine you are in the shower and think, "I should reach out to Mike and let him know he's doing a great job. I haven't spoken with him in a while, and I owe him a call." If you don't add *Call Mike and check in* to your to-do list immediately, it will likely be forgotten, overridden by competing thoughts, before you step out of the shower.

The format and mechanism by which you maintain a to-do list is up to you, but choose something readily available and easily edited. I find a smartphone works perfectly for keeping lists, but a journal, notepad, or voice recorder would also do the trick.

I was once in a meeting with a CEO when the conversation meandered and we ended up discussing vacation destinations. He said he would send me the name of a small village he once visited in Europe. I didn't expect him to actually send me the name of the village; his comment seemed like one of those things that people say, and he probably said a thousand things that day. Later that evening, he sent me an email from the plane with the name of the village and some additional details. That CEO said what he was going to do, wrote it down on his list of open action items, held himself accountable, and took care of the task. No matter how trivial a task might seem, the act of writing it down and crossing it off your list gives you a sense of accomplishment and differentiates you from ninety percent of people who have good intentions but forget about the little things. Keeping a to-do list and getting things done are key traits shared by great leaders.

Secret 23: If You See a Problem, Fix the Problem

Imagine returning from a long week of traveling. You took the red-eye flight home, and you are exhausted. All you want to do is go to bed. That's exactly what most people in this situation will do; go straight to bed. But by going to bed, you're not addressing some problems. Your suitcase isn't unpacked, your dirty clothes from the trip are still squashed in your bag, your blood pressure medicine is buried in a toiletry bag, and your laptop needs charging. What if you were to stay awake an extra thirty minutes to unpack your suitcase, take a shower, program the coffee maker, plug in your laptop, and throw your clothes in the washing machine? You would probably sleep better knowing everything was taken care of, and you would have more time to ease into the morning the next day.

Problems don't age well. As a leader, you are obligated to act fast and address problems as soon as you see them. Allowing them to fester inevitably makes them worse. You will never hear somebody say, "I wish I had waited longer to address that problem."

Secret 24: **Treat Everyone Like Family**

Too often, leaders are moving fast and treating people like tools in their tool bag or weapons in their arsenal. It's easy to view a short, casual interaction with an employee as trivial, but that person likely took everything you said to heart in what might be the only conversation the person has with you that week.

As a leader, your words carry weight and have a significant impact on people's morale, demeanor, and engagement. Quickly dismissing or chastising a low-performing employee might be tempting, but that person is probably hungry for coaching, advice, and guidance and definitely does not want to be a low performer. Maybe the low-performing employee is going through a personal struggle or was dealt an unfair hand by you or your predecessor. Before chastising, imagine this person is your father, mother, sister, or brother. How would you want your family treated? Looking at daily interactions through this lens changes everything. Your people are not objects. They deserve to be treated with empathy and respect. The greatest leader you have ever worked for understands this principle.

Secret 25: **Show No Fear**

Fear is an unavoidable and essential part of the human experience. Without it, we might nonchalantly walk into a bear's cave and become its dinner. Although *experiencing* fear is unavoidable, *showing* fear is a choice. Would you follow a general into battle who looks terrified? Would you get on an airplane with a scared pilot? Great leaders experience fear but never let you know it in the moment (hence the term "fearless leader"). Part of being a great leader is being genuine and authentic, however, so you often hear great leaders admitting that they were afraid after the fact.

One of my greatest fears was speaking in front of very large groups of people. When I was asked to present on stage the night before a huge, company-wide event, internally I was terrified, but outwardly I smiled and said, "Absolutely! I would love to. Thanks for asking me to do it." I didn't sleep at all that night and spent hours practicing my speech and rehearsing my body language. The next morning, I got mic'd up backstage, heard my cue, and stepped out under the blinding lights before a sea of thousands of people. I faced one of my biggest fears with confidence and actually enjoyed the experience. After stepping off the stage, people said things like, "You're so lucky that stuff doesn't bother you. I could never do that!" and "You crushed it! You looked so comfortable up there." I admitted to those people that I was actually terrified and wouldn't have dared attempt it without ample preparation. Once you've looked your biggest fear in the eyes and prevailed, you feel unstoppable. When it comes to fear, the "fake it 'til you make it" adage works perfectly. Act as if you have no fear, and you will become fearless.

Secret 26: **Be grateful**

It's so easy to fall down a rabbit hole of negativity and forget how fortunate you are. Leaders who carry themselves with gratitude are magnets for positivity. The best leaders I know thank people for their time, their presence, and their hard work. Being grateful for others is contagious and creates a culture of appreciation. People who feel appreciated often do more than is asked or expected of them. Gratitude and appreciation comes in many forms; it can be expressed monetarily, verbally, or through public praise and recognition.

Secret 27: **Be Kind**

I once found myself having lunch at a restaurant with a sales manager who was rude to the waiter. He scolded the waiter for taking so long with our food, and he was condescending throughout the meal. I'm not sure if he thought I would be impressed by his behavior, but I couldn't have been more disgusted. I would never do business with somebody who acts that way. A kind leader is not a weak leader. Having empathy for people, genuinely caring about their well-being and helping them achieve success without degrading or berating them, actually takes more time, effort, and emotional intelligence than the alternative. Being a kind leader doesn't mean you foster a "soft" culture that lets people skate by with subpar performance. It means you are a good person who knows how to hold people accountable and drive performance by using more advanced motivation techniques. Some of the wealthiest and most successful people I know are also some of the most well-mannered, polite, and humble people I know. I don't think that's a coincidence.

Secret 28: **Own It**

If not you, then who? Great leaders never need to be asked to lead; they just do it. People debate about whether leaders are born with the instinct to lead or acquire a sense of obligation through their life experiences, but either way, something inside a leader screams, "If I don't do this, nobody will. If not me, then who?"

When I was a sales leader in New York City, I had a couple of open spots on my team so I decided to host a mini career fair in our office. I hired a caterer, promoted the event, gathered résumés, and assembled a group of hiring managers to meet with prospective candidates. Dozens of people signed up to attend. I scheduled the event to start at 6 p.m. to allow people enough time to leave their other jobs (if they had other jobs) and get to our office. A late start also gave me some time to make sure the office was presentable and ready to accept guests.

Growing up, when we were expecting company, my family ran around making sure everything was shipshape before guests arrived. I felt the same sense of urgency when inviting people into our office space. I wanted to make a good impression on our prospective employees and ensure that our company was well-represented. It was the end of a long workday and the usual detritus was strewn about the office: discarded coffee cups, crumbs on the floor, misplaced charging cables, etc. I went to the maintenance closet, found a vacuum cleaner, and began cleaning the carpets. I sensed people watching me, so I looked up and saw shocked faces from a handful of coworkers. They asked in disbelief, "Why are you vacuuming? That's not your job!" When I have a goal, my job is to remove all obstacles standing in the way of achieving that goal, and so everything is my job. The floor had crumbs on it and needed vacuuming.

Ultimately, the event was a big success. We had a great turnout, met some interesting people, and identified a handful of top candidates. We interviewed our top choices and made offers on the spot. We hired five people at that event, and they went on to have long and successful careers with the company.

Taking initiative and stepping up to a task is not the same as being a lone wolf or doing people's jobs for them. The fact is, Human Resources would have needed a lot of time to plan a career fair like this; they would need to fly people in, find local vendors, work with marketing on promoting it, have meetings, review with other departments, and so on.

Finding someone to clean the floor would have taken a lot longer than giving it a quick vacuum myself. Sometimes if you want something done quickly, taking the reins and doing it yourself is the best option. That doesn't mean doing it all alone. I enlisted the help of other local hiring managers, we delegated tasks, and everyone chipped in to make it a successful event.

It's okay to delegate tasks as a leader; you can't do it all. Delegating tasks to free up time for other tasks is not shirking your responsibility. Using your time and the time of others in the most efficient manner is your obligation as a leader. But nothing is beneath you, and you should always be willing to step in and own it!

Listen for the phrase "That's not my job." You will be surprised how many times you hear it thrown around the workplace. Once I recognized that people viewed themselves as having a specific set of siloed tasks from which they shouldn't deviate, I established a new mandate for my team: your job is everything and anything that moves the team closer to our goal.

Great things happen when people remove the artificial limitations of job descriptions from their mindsets. It's empowering to be told, "Your job is anything that contributes to the success of the team and the company." People are more inclined to work together as a cohesive team if they know they are all working toward a common goal. If it's nobody's job, it's everybody's job.

Secret 29: **Define a vision**

Visualization is one of the most underrated tools in our tool bags. Great leaders have clear visions and are always working toward them. Working toward your vision also means having a plan to get there. A vision without a plan is a dream. Leading is impossible if you don't know where you are going. Great leaders share their visions, they talk about them often, they solicit feedback, and they encourage input.

Having a vision fosters excitement and unity. I like to literally share my vision with my team by creating a vision board with pictures of what we are trying to achieve. It might sound corny, but I have achieved 100 percent of the visions I've depicted in this way. When you have a clear vision, you are unstoppable. When you are unstoppable, you can achieve anything. Manifesting your wildest dreams is not only possible, but highly likely, when you focus on them, talk about them, think about them, and involve others. The more specific and measurable your vision is, the more likely you are to achieve it.

My first year in college, I was distracted, not studying enough, and my grades began to slip. I decided to get serious about studying and work toward a vision. I printed pictures of a nice house, a nice car, a swimming pool, and a custom suit on a piece of paper. I carried that piece of paper in my wallet for the rest of my college career (Fig. 4). Any time I was tempted to stop studying and go partying, I would remember what I was working toward. I kept that paper in my wallet after I graduated and entered the workforce. Achieving everything on that paper took me a few years, but I never forgot what I was working toward and went on to achieve everything I had envisioned. I continued to raise the bar and set higher goals, not just tangible and monetary goals, but anything my mind could conjure. This is the underlying architecture of growth: raise the bar, achieve it, set a higher bar, and repeat.

Fig. 4. My actual vision board from college.

Visualization isn't limited to positive outcomes. Visualizing negative outcomes (temporarily) is a great way to mitigate unfortunate scenarios; it helps you identify potential pitfalls and make plans to avoid them. In simpler terms, hope for the best, plan for the worst. In sales, a negative visualization might be "If we don't overachieve against our quota this quarter, the company could miss earning targets, which could drive down the stock price" or "If I don't get this deal at the bank, we could lose credibility across the entire financial services vertical."

When I wrote this book, I visualized positive outcomes, like good reviews and good sales. I also visualized negative outcomes, like bad reviews and poor sales. I visualized potential feedback and wrote hypothetical book reviews. I then used the reviews to edit and revise the book. Here are the reviews I visualized, some positive and some negative:

Loved it! I learned a lot about what it takes to be a successful leader. There are actionable tips and great advice that I can immediately put to use in the real world. I found myself reinvigorated and filled with motivation to get to work! I highly recommend this book and will be giving a copy to everyone on my team!

Pretty good. I learned a few things and I was entertained by some of the stories. I saw some similarities to my own journey and I think people who are just getting into leadership would get a lot out of this book.

★ ★ ★

It was okay. A lot of this stuff is common sense. I picked up a few nuggets that I can use, but for the most part, it's just like all the other leadership books on the market. Good news though—it was a pretty quick read. Banged it out in a few hours.

★ ★

I do not recommend this book. It was filled with mostly useless information. Save your money and watch some online tutorials if you want to learn about sales leadership.

Awful! This book is a self-absorbed pile of garbage. I didn't learn anything at all, plus it was poorly written, riddled with grammatical errors, and doesn't apply to my industry.

By visualizing a range of potential outcomes, I was able to tweak the book and directly address the hypothetical feedback. The reality is, we can't control the world and we can't please everyone, but we can do our best to focus on what is within our control and plan for a range of potential outcomes.

Secret 30: **Build Big Teams Around You**

Even the President of the United States needs help. He has advisors, a cabinet, and resources upon whom he can rely. Like most difficult tasks in life, leading can't be done alone. Great sales leaders surround themselves with like-minded, self-motivated people who are all swimming in the same direction and working toward a common goal. Like a football coach who positions players on a field to win a game, great sales leaders position their teams for success by aligning the players' skill sets with the right resources.

Some of the most effective teams I've built in my career were comprised of people from a wide array of backgrounds, skill sets, and functions. It is absolutely appropriate for sales leaders to enlist the help of people outside their organization (marketing, operations, product management, finance, etc.). If anyone declines to join the effort or has a "that's not my job" attitude, keep moving; you don't want those people on your team.

Success begets success, winners want to be around winners, and people are drawn to great leaders. Once a reputation of achievement is established, the problem is no longer finding people to join your team; the problem becomes the overwhelming number of people who want to hitch their wagons to your success.

Secret 31: **Stay Calm**

As a leader, your patience and your boundaries will be tested. Issues will bubble up and you will face some very challenging situations and decisions. When children test their parents, both the children and the parents are best served if the parents take a calm and peaceful approach. The same applies to great leaders—much like they show no fear, they also never blow up. Somebody once told me, "It only takes one blowup to drain the whole reservoir." In the case of leadership, the metaphorical reservoir is filled with goodwill. If you remain levelheaded and measured before responding, people will view you as a sensible, thoughtful leader whom they can rely on during the most challenging times.

If you feel yourself losing your cool, think about ducks. A duck glides smoothly across the surface of the water, but if you could see what was happening below the calm surface, you would see two duck feet feverishly paddling. Always stay calm on the surface, even if your inner duck feet are racing.

Staying calm in written communication is also important because it serves as a permanent record of your demeanor and tone. Always proofread written communications at least three times before sending. My chief legal counsel at a previous job once said, "Don't put anything in writing unless you would be comfortable seeing it displayed on a large screen in front of a jury in size seventy-two font."

Knee-jerk responses or strongly worded emails might feel good to send, but they are never a good idea. My rule of thumb when sending emails is "if in doubt, throw it out." If you are second-guessing an email, then you already know in your gut that it's a bad idea, so don't send it.

Great leaders always take the high road and never resort to yelling, intimidation, or name calling. Calm heads always prevail, and calm leaders achieve great things.

Secret 32: **Give Back**

If you are fortunate enough to find yourself in a position of leadership, you have an obligation to set an example and give something back. Giving back comes in many forms, and it's a very personal decision. You could join the board of a local nonprofit organization, donate your time to a local food pantry, walk dogs at an animal shelter, or contribute to any other cause that is near and dear to you. Including your team and peers in your philanthropic endeavors increases your overall impact and introduces others to the gift of giving.

Giving back also means reaching back down the corporate ladder and mentoring people who might not have had the same opportunities you've encountered. Think of all of the mistakes you've made and lessons you've learned on the way to leadership. You could shorten others' ramps to success and give people chances you never had. Reach out to schools to ask if their career or guidance departments are looking for guest speakers. Volunteer to review résumés or conduct mock interviews for people trying to get their lives on track. If you aren't sure where to start or how to give back, just reflect on the early days of your career. What do you wish somebody had done for you? Whatever that thing is, do it!

Secret 33: **Respect the Calendar**

Time is our most precious resource. As a leader, you have the ability to manage people's calendars, and that is a responsibility you should not take lightly. Never ask your team to spend time doing anything you wouldn't do. Find ways to shorten meetings, use fewer words, and cut back on small talk. When people take time off for vacation or to be with their families, do not contact them, no matter how important it feels to you in the moment. The employee you called for a quick question was at her daughter's graduation. She saw you calling and felt obligated to pick up because you're her boss. Her moment of pride and joy was interrupted, not only by you, but by the associated flood of thoughts and feelings she experienced when her mind shifted into work mode. That employee's special family moment was just ambushed by your unwittingly disrespectful phone call, and her memories from that day are forever tarnished by your intrusion.

Vacations are not the only time you should leave people alone; weekends are also sacred. Sending an email to your team on a weekend might seem harmless, but getting a written communication from your boss can ruin a weekend. If I receive an email on a Sunday, I might not feel compelled to respond, but when I hear the notification, I will glance at my email to make sure there's no emergency. Just seeing the correspondence fills my mind with thoughts of work and outstanding items that need my attention. I become aggravated with the sender's lack of respect for my time, and in turn, I lose respect for the sender.

Secret 34: **Think Big**

Set audacious goals, create a vision, build a plan to get there, and manifest it into reality with your team. The bigger you think, the more you will achieve. To think big, you must remove all mental constraints and artificial limitations. For example, if you have a $100 million revenue quota this year, put a plan together to reach $300 million in revenue. Even if you miss by $100 million, you still will have achieved 200 percent of your quota.

Secret 35: Work *On* the Business, Not *In* the Business

One of the traps most new leaders fall into is reverting back to what they know and do best—rolling up their sleeves and getting directly involved in the business. Running the deals, setting strategy, and having your arms around the business feels good, but that's not the place for a leader. Leaders can't scale if they are too involved in the day-to-day operations. Your job is to work on the business. Ensure the right players are on the field at the right time with the right tools and game plan to win. Your job is to coach your players, not play the game for them.

Secret 36: Make Clear Decisions From a Distance

Leaders often find themselves in the position of mediator or arbiter. Conflicts arise within the team and bubble up to you for input, resolution, and judgment. The closer to an issue a person is, the more emotion involved, so your team needs your help as an objective third party. They are too close to the conflict to think rationally or objectively. Your job as a leader is to keep your emotions out of these situations and make clear decisions based on facts. You will never make everyone happy—it's impossible—but consistently doing the right thing based on a set of well-defined and advertised principles makes conflict resolution and decision-making an easy part of the leadership role.

Secret 37: **Give and Solicit Feedback**

Feedback is a gift that can change the trajectory of someone's career. Nobody wants to keep doing things that are setting them back. As a leader, your responsibility is to help people discover their blind spots by having candid conversations and providing them with constructive feedback. At the beginning of each fiscal year, I host an all-hands meeting where I lay out initiatives, review our plan for success, and set expectations. At the end of the meeting, I share areas where I think I can improve, and I invite everyone interested in participating in a customized, private feedback exercise to reach out to me. Receiving feedback can be ego-shattering, and most people don't want to hear it, but I usually get a handful of people who ask to participate in the feedback exercise. I start by asking them for the names of fifteen people they work with on a regular basis. I send the following email to ten of the people:

Hi, Joe. I am working with Priscilla on a career development and brand awareness exercise. You have been selected as someone who works with Priscilla and could provide valuable feedback.

Please take a moment to provide honest and direct answers to the three questions below. This feedback will be collected and shared with Priscilla anonymously (your name will not be mentioned) as part of Priscilla's ongoing career and brand development.

Please reply with the following three data points as they relate to your interactions with Priscilla.

1. What is one word you would use to describe Priscilla?
2. Please complete the following sentence: Priscilla is great, but _____.
3. Please share any other observations, comments, or feedback for Priscilla.

Thank you,
Adam

Once I receive all the responses, I compile the feedback, anonymize it, and review it with the people seeking feedback. We talk about the common themes, trends, and points made, and then we decide if we agree or disagree. I then ask them to place themselves on a talent quadrant (Fig. 5). The x-axis rates their perceived brand from poor (far left) to exceptional (far right), and the y-axis rates their job performance from poor (bottom) to exceptional (top). In simple terms, a very unsuccessful sales rep who acts like a jerk would fall squarely in the D quadrant.

Once we agree on their quadrant placement, we discuss plans to elevate their brand and address the feedback. Somebody that is viewed as too serious, for example, might want to host a fun team trivia game or a happy hour to show a lighter side. Somebody who is viewed as selfish might want to share a best practice with the team.

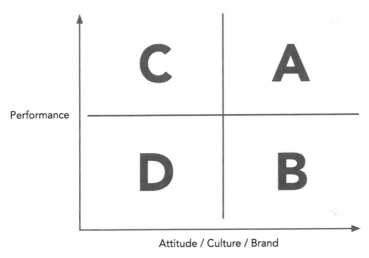

Fig. 5. Talent quadrant.

As leaders, we tend to spend too much time with people in the A quadrant because A players are the most fun to be with. They are successful, active, and doing all the right things. However, we should instead focus on helping others get into the A quadrant. Focus the bulk of your time on getting B and C players into the A quadrant through coaching, feedback, and development. Generally, the D players with a poor attitude and poor performance are not coachable and should be replaced and upgraded.

Just as you offer feedback to your team, you should solicit feedback for yourself and share your shortcomings with your team. Tell them you are a work in progress, come up with a scorecard, rate yourself, tell the team where you think you can improve, and ask if they agree. Admitting that you are far from perfect and need help just like everyone else is a powerfully humble statement.

Secret 38: Set Goals That Are Time Bound and Measurable

Most people set vague goals. In January, ask friends if they made New Year's resolutions. You will hear answers like "I want to get healthy." The problem is that "getting healthy" is a vague goal; it has no time limit or success criteria, and the definition of *healthy* is subject to opinion. A better goal would be "I want to lose ten pounds in the next two months." This goal is bound by time (two months) and can be measured (ten pounds).

In business, people set goals all the time and often fall into the same trap. "I want to grow my business 20 percent this year." Technically, that is a goal, but it is also an outcome. Growing your business 20 percent would be the outcome of achieving other goals and milestones along the way. A better way to set a 20-percent growth goal would be, "I want to grow my business 20 percent within the next twelve months by realizing 30 percent of our annual bookings in the first quarter, increasing our win rate by 10 percent, and achieving a sales rep participation rate of 75 percent by the end of the first half."

Goals don't materialize without a plan. Every goal you set as a leader must be accompanied by a plan to get there, including tactics and strategy. Your entire team needs to understand the mission and the plan so they can align their individual actions and goals to yours. While external factors might force you to change the way you get to your goal, the mission should not change.

Secret 39: Inspect What You Expect

If you expect your team members to meet with three new clients a week, have you told them that? Are you checking their activity? Are you looking at their calendars? Are you coaching them on getting new meetings? Are your cross-functional teams helping? What resources are being leveraged? How are the meetings going? Are three meetings a week a realistic target? Just hoping that something is happening without inspecting it is like trying to land a plane with your eyes closed and hoping everything will be okay. Hope is not a strategy, and you can't expect what you don't inspect. Your team needs to understand what "good" looks like, and they should never be surprised to hear that they are not meeting your expectations.

Secret 40: **Family First**

Family always comes before work. As a leader, the quickest way to alienate and lose great people is by forcing them to choose between their family and their career. You never know what goes on in people's homes and the challenges they face outside of work. We ask a lot from our people; we need to respect the boundary between their work and home lives.

A salesperson's spouse often makes significant sacrifices. The job of a sales rep usually requires odd hours, late nights, extensive travel, and lots of time away from family. At the end of each quarter, I take the top sales rep and his or her spouse out for a dinner at a restaurant of their choosing. At these appreciation dinners, I focus on the spouse, not the rep. I thank them for enabling their partner's success by making sacrifices at home, just like my mother made sacrifices to enable my father's career. I recognize the rep's achievements and speak in glowing terms about their accomplishments. I order the wine (the good stuff that's hard to pronounce), and I give them a night to remember. The notes I get after those dinners are some of my favorites. Not only do the sales reps feel appreciated, but their spouses are so grateful to be involved and touched that somebody took the time to acknowledge the sacrifices they have made behind the scenes.

Most of us work to support our families. They are the reason we get up, get out, and get uncomfortable every day. Family always comes first.

SIX

THE TOUCHSTONE LEADER

You've probably encountered an exceptional leader in your career, somebody who always seemed to know what to do, remained calm in difficult or stressful situations, was beloved by the team, and fearlessly propelled the team toward greatness.

Think about that person in your life. Picture the person's face, voice, and demeanor. For the sake of this conversation, we will call that person Fred. Rather than thinking about Fred as an individual person, let's consider him an amalgamation of great leaders: Francine, Richard, Emma, and Dave (**FRED**). Asking yourself the question "What would Fred do in this situation?" is like calling a friend for advice, but instead of picking up the phone, you peruse a mental catalog of Fred's guiding principles to filter and vet decisions through.

In other words, Fred is a touchstone against which you can test, compare, and measure your own leadership decisions and attributes. The word touchstone comes from a time when a literal stone was used to compare the marks made by various metals. It was a benchmark against which every metal was compared. In the context of leadership, you can think of Fred as a touchstone, an established leadership benchmark that you can contrast your actions and decisions against.

While occasionally checking in against a benchmark can be an effective tool for self-improvement, constantly comparing yourself to somebody else can lead to feelings of inadequacy and frustration. Don't try to impersonate Fred. You aren't Fred; you can only be you. Instead, think of Fred like an owner's manual. You are simply recalling his decision-making process based on the data set that you've been exposed to, and you're mentally "asking" him for advice.

Looking up to and emulating role models is not a revolutionary concept, but doing so effectively while being true to yourself can be a precarious balancing act. I've seen people over rotate and exhibit extreme Fred impersonation. Imitating somebody's personality is not the same as emulating the person's behaviors; the former usually comes across as unnatural and disingenuous.

I once worked for a VP of sales I'll call Steve. Steve was beloved and revered. He was a strong person, a great leader, calm under pressure, and somebody you wanted in your corner. One day, Steve left the company to work for a competitor. In the months that followed Steve's departure, a new VP of sales emerged who was clearly trying to channel Steve's energy, demeanor, and mannerisms. Steve had a deep, gruff voice, and he exhibited unique physical behaviors, like clapping his hands for emphasis. The new VP clearly wanted to be revered and respected like Steve because he was literally doing an impression of him. The problem was that Steve's mannerisms did not fit the new VP's personality; he seemed uncomfortable clapping his hands and trying to gruff up his voice.

Steve's approach was unique and suited him well, but just as retelling the joke of a professional stand-up comedian rarely has the same comedic timing and impact, imitating a great leader rarely has the same motivational effect. Seeking inspiration and guidance from a great leader is not the same thing as trying to be somebody else. If all else fails, be yourself and trust your gut.

I have a specific leader whom I think about often when faced with a challenging or complicated situation. I ask myself, "What would Fred do?" Fred seemed to have all the answers, but he wasn't arrogant or egotistical. He just had extreme confidence and steadfastness in his decision-making abilities. Fred trusted his gut and remained calm under pressure. His confidence came from years of experience, introspection, and self-awareness; he knew exactly who he was and what he stood for, and as a result, he could handle anything that came his way. He had a strong moral compass and a willingness to learn. He always put the interests of others before himself.

I worked directly for Fred once, and he gave me a gift. That gift was feedback. He pulled me into a room and asked me if I knew my "buts." In other words, Adam is great, but _____. I did not know my "buts," but he did. "Adam is great, but he is too intense and should smile more. Adam is great, but he's not approachable." This feedback was tough to hear but greatly appreciated. I had no idea people perceived me that way. I was never a natural smiler; my resting face looked pretty serious, which was coming across as standoffish and intense. I asked Fred what I could do to change people's minds, and he suggested some low-effort, high-visibility activities that would expose people to a different side of me.

Fred booked a conference room with a video camera and worked with me on a script. Recently I had closed a deal in a new market segment, and so Fred wanted to record me walking through what I did and sharing best practices with the team. He had me do multiple takes, saying things like, "Let's do it again, but relax your shoulders and smile this time." Fred sent the final video clip to his entire organization with the message "Team, please take a moment to watch this best practice that Adam wants to share with the broader team."

The result was incredible. People thanked me for taking the time to share lessons learned. With that video, I was suddenly perceived as more approachable; I know, because people literally began approaching me!

I learned two valuable lessons that day. First, take the time to gift the gift of feedback. If people don't know their "buts," they can't take control of their brand. Second, perception is reality. If people think you are an intense, cranky, unapproachable jerk, then you are until proven otherwise. To this day, when I see somebody unknowingly self-destructing, I think about what Fred did for me and offer the person candid feedback and recommended corrective action.

As a leader, you have found yourself in the fortunate position of having a platform, which comes with a responsibility to elevate others and guide the way for future leaders. As much as we should think about what

Fred would do, it is equally important to think about what Fred wouldn't do. Fred wouldn't over-imbibe at the holiday party. He wouldn't post pictures of his new Porsche on social media. He wouldn't send sarcastic or passive-aggressive emails. He wouldn't engage in gossip or speak behind people's backs. If you are doing things that Fred would not do, stop!

Generally, Fred is somebody you enjoy being around. He is easygoing, smiles a lot, and is somebody you would like to get a beer with. If you want to see how you compare to Fred, you can do a simple exercise. Take out a piece of paper or flip to exercise #2 in the back of the book. Write down ten words that you feel best describe you. Then, turn the paper over and write down ten words that best describe your favorite person to spend time with. I did this exercise many years ago and it was eye opening.

My ten words:

1. Competitive
2. Persistent
3. Tenacious
4. Assertive
5. Thoughtful
6. Detail-oriented
7. Consistent
8. Accountable
9. Reliable
10. Compassionate

My favorite person's ten words:

1. Humble
2. Kind
3. Funny
4. Loving
5. Sympathetic
6. Relaxed
7. Spontaneous
8. Adventurous
9. Generous
10. Ambitious

You might find, like I did, that your ten words look nothing like the ten words that describe your favorite person to spend time with. This was a life-changing exercise for me. The attributes that I thought were helping me progress in the world were not aligned with the attributes I (and presumably other people) wanted to surround myself with. If you have similar results, I recommend choosing a few words from your favorite person's list and making a daily effort to showcase those characteristics to other people.

You might not know it, but right now you are somebody's Fred. Somebody is watching you from afar with great admiration. Someone might be lurking in the back of a room learning from your speech patterns and interactions. Set a great example and be the kind of person that people want to be around.

SEVEN

ACQUIRE, BUILD, AND RUN

You might have landed your current leadership position in a variety of ways. Maybe you were a successful sales rep who just wanted to try something new. Perhaps you stuck around long enough that when the right people left, it was your turn to take the reins. Possibly you always saw yourself as a leader, built a plan, interviewed well, and landed a new role. Regardless of how you found yourself in the position, you are now a sales leader and are likely faced with the challenge of acquiring, building, and running an existing team.

ACQUIRE

When most people hear the word acquire, they think of purchasing something, as in "I acquired a new home." Acquiring something makes you the owner of it, which is why we use this term to describe taking ownership of a new team. As a newly appointed sales leader, you now own your sales team (for better or worse). As we talked about in Chapter 4, you should already have a plan or idea of what this specific team needs. No two teams are alike, and every single individual impacts the dynamic of the team. Just like one bad apple ruins the bunch, one negative rep can taint the entire team. Acquiring a team successfully is impossible without doing some research beforehand; you must know what you are acquiring so you can prepare and tweak your approach.

It could be that you are acquiring a seasoned, top-performing team of motivated self-starters who work well together and need little direction. Or perhaps you are tasked with hiring a brand-new team at a start-up. In other cases you might inherit somebody else's problem, perhaps a team of dysfunctional, jaded, apathetic sellers. Let's explore two extremely different scenarios and discuss best practices and communication strategies to ensure the smoothest acquisition while delivering near-term buy-in and long-term results.

We'll start with the "seasoned, top-performing team of motivated self-starters who work well together and need little direction." On paper, this team sounds easy to acquire, but it is actually one of the most challenging teams to lead. On the surface, nothing is broken. Results are being delivered, and by all accounts, the team doesn't need to be managed. So what's the problem?

The problem lies in the team's success. Teams in this category are often satisfied with their current levels of achievement and resist any change, even if it could result in additional growth opportunities. High-performing sellers can be impervious to new ideas. They can often be combative and lack operational cadence. Like with any team, your first step as a leader is to establish clear expectations for them and you. Your messaging out of the gate must be crystal clear with no room for interpretation but also mixed with hints of self-awareness and gratitude. If I was acquiring this team, my day-one message would sound something like this:

> You all have achieved great things, and it's an honor to join such a well-established, high-performing team with a stellar reputation. It is the sales leader's responsibility to help you achieve even more by removing obstacles and working tirelessly toward even greater horizons to better

serve our customers and shareholders and to ensure continued success for you and your families. There is so much we can learn from each other, and there is zero doubt that we are going to do even greater things than you have imagined.

Notice I didn't use the words *I* or *me* once in this communication. Being a sales leader is never about you; it is about the team. I started by acknowledging their established success and the groundwork they have already laid. I set clear expectations for the role of the leader and the sellers. I mentioned their families and encouraged them to "imagine." I told them I can learn from them, but I was also clear that they can learn from me. All of these are key words that disarm and perk up skeptical reps. I acknowledged the team's historical success but made it clear that we are focused on even greater future success. You can see the importance of choosing your words carefully, especially in the very beginning. So many leaders immediately alienate new teams by focusing on their own personal achievements and not the success of the teams.

Remember, even a high-performing team has a top-performing rep and a bottom-performing rep. The distance between your top rep and your bottom rep is where your opportunity to make a meaningful impact lies.

ACQUIRE, BUILD, AND RUN

Next, let's look at the very different team known as "dys-functional, jaded, apathetic sellers." Taking on this team might fill you with nervousness or even dread. Expecting the worst, based on the team's reputation, would be an understandable instinct.

During high school, I worked at an animal hospital. The hospital doubled as a boarding kennel where people dropped their pets to be cared for when they were away from home. As a result, we saw some animals on a regular basis and became familiar with their idiosyncrasies. On each animal's cage, we hung a card with the animal's key information (name, breed, diet, medication, etc.). If the animal was dangerous and shouldn't be approached, we also attached a sticker that cautioned in large, bright orange letters, "WILL BITE." I remember a poodle named Duncan that always arrived muzzled. He was ushered into his cage like Hannibal Lecter, and the big, orange sticker was quickly affixed. I once found myself alone with Duncan on a quiet summer day, and we caught each other's eyes. He didn't look mean, and I found it hard to believe that he would actually bite anyone. I slipped a treat through the bars, and he gobbled it up. I slipped him a couple more treats throughout the next few days, and soon he became excited to see me. I mustered up the courage to pet him on the head, and eventually we became friends. Duncan never bit me, and I never saw any vicious tendencies in him. He was just misunderstood. People never took the time to work with him because they were influenced by the preconceived idea that he was a vicious biter.

When acquiring a team with a bad reputation, forming your own opinion of them is important. Try to ignore the "WILL BITE" sticker. With such a team, go in with eyes wide open and ears in listening mode. The team already knows they are not performing, and they are likely bracing for a micromanager who will criticize everything or fire everybody. You can surprise them by giving them an opportunity to embrace new ideas and thrive under your leadership. If I was acquiring this struggling team, my early communication would go something like this:

> We are going to roll up our sleeves and get this team to where we all know it can and should be. It is going to be hard work, but you have demonstrated tenacity and a willingness to work hard, so there is no doubt that we are going to be successful together. We are going to get out there, implement some new strategies, and look back on this time as a necessary step on our journey toward greatness.

Just like with any team, your messaging and words should be focused on them and not yourself. You don't need to point out their shortcomings. They are painfully aware and are looking for a savior to guide them out of the current situation, into the promised land. Be focused on the future, not the past. Your use of optimism and enthusiasm are the dog whistles and call to action your top performers have been waiting for. This team likely has fundamental issues and will need personnel changes and upgrades, but in the first thirty days you need to be in observation mode to see for yourself where the problems lie and whether or not these dogs really do bite.

BUILD

In some cases, you need to build a team rather than acquire it. In other cases, you acquire a team only to learn that some degree of building or rebuilding is required. Sales leaders usually favor building a team versus acquiring one because they have more control over the makeup of the team and they can bring in "their people" who are already committed. The people they hire come with a sense of loyalty and gratitude to the hiring manager. The downside of building is that it takes longer to ramp up and comes with more uncertainty.

If you find yourself building a team, relaying a very clear vision of where you are going is critical. Treat your team like you are operating an independent business and you are the CEO. Your business should have a mission statement that serves as a North Star, an unwavering set of guiding principles and definition of purpose. From interviews to onboarding, people need to know exactly what they are signing up for and if they can envision themselves playing a role in your journey. If people aren't clear on the team's vision, they won't know if they are a good fit. Having a vision also provides you with the mental clarity required to hire the right people needed to be successful.

Some sales reps are great at farming existing accounts but struggle with acquiring net new customers or hunting for new business. When building a team, you are more likely looking for hunters, especially in high-growth start-up environments where the success of the company hinges on the consistent acquisition of new logos. Conversely, some teams might have specific target accounts that are a good match for their products or services, and so they need to hire reps with established contacts and relationships to break into those accounts.

To treat your team like a business, give the team its own name, brand, identity, culture, and logo. I once acquired an underperforming team in New York City. When I asked them what they wanted to be known for, their answers were all similar: winning, being competitive, being aggressive, and the like. Based on that discussion, the team and I coauthored the mission statement, "To provide our customers with a world-class experience through our dedication to making their lives easier by providing a superior product and service that drives profitability for our company." We came up with a name for our team and created a sharp logo that we added to all of our presentations. I had a photographer come into the office to take professional headshots with a consistent background. We were the only sales team in the company that had headshots in our internal directory profiles. Everybody felt a sense of pride and ownership. We had coauthored our mission, and we all took responsibility for the integrity of our brand.

Once you have a clear brand, you can reinforce and promote it in many ways. For example, when looking to hire, most hiring managers post job openings on professional networking sites like LinkedIn and list all the attributes they are seeking in the ideal candidates, such as ten years of relevant experience, proven track record of success, and so on. Posts like these are so commonplace they often get overlooked or garner only a few interactions. A cool little trick you can use to promote your brand and culture is instead of posting what you *do* want, post what you *don't* want. When I post a job listing, I use it as an opportunity to signal my brand and what I care about to both current and prospective employees. Here's one of my recent job postings:

Great opportunity for an inspirational leader to work with an awesome team of seasoned sellers! Please DO NOT APPLY if you are a micromanager who uses fear and intimidation to drive results.

My intent with this post was threefold. First, I wanted to get noticed. The post stands out from the normal, boring job postings. Second, I wanted to send a clear message to the public that culture is important and I won't tolerate jerks. Third, I wanted my existing team to see the post and feel proud that I called them seasoned. They were grateful that I understood the kind of leader they needed to thrive, and they appreciated that I was protecting the team culture that we worked so hard to create.

The same trick can be used to promote other leaders when they are hiring a sales rep. In another post, I projected our company brand and leadership expectations while endorsing the hiring manager and helping to attract top talent:

Troy isn't a manager; he's a coach and a mentor who thrives on the success of his team. If you want to join Troy and play a major role in transforming an industry, this is the place to be!

Every time you add a new person to a team, the dynamic changes but your mission stays the same. Your job as a sales leader and hiring manager is to ensure that the productivity of your team is not adversely impacted by new additions and that you are not distracted from your purpose...all while getting your new addition up to speed and productive in the shortest amount of time possible.

Think of your team as a human body in need of a kidney transplant. If the new kidney is not a perfect match for the body, the patient could experience organ rejection and the kidney could potentially damage other parts of the body. When building a team, hiring is everything. It's okay if you get it wrong; it's not okay to let the problem fester. If the patient is experiencing organ failure, remove the bad kidney and replace it with a better match as soon as possible.

Keep in mind, moving problems is not the same as resolving problems. If you want to remove an employee from your team, providing them with a recommendation to join a different team at your company is not helpful. Doing so does not solve a problem; it moves a problem, which only delays the inevitable.

RUN

Once you have successfully acquired or built your team, the truly rewarding and fun part of leading a sales team begins. Your team is already aligned with your vision (you made sure of that when you acquired or hired them), you have everyone rowing in the same direction, and now your job is to keep things running smoothly. When the machine is running, you can move faster, anticipate curves in the road ahead, and bask in the spoils of building while you grow. The key to keeping a team running while simultaneously growing is Accountability, Recognition, and Consistency (ARC).

Accountability

Sales reps understand that they live by the sword and die by the sword. In sales, the sword is bookings, attainment, and results. If a salesperson isn't selling, then they are out of a job. The primary responsibility of the sales leader is to help reps sell by holding them accountable to specific targets and metrics. If reps are unclear as to what is expected, they can't hold themselves accountable.

A lot of sales leaders only share historical metrics, but reporting the news is not as valuable as creating the news. Sharing historical data like bookings, sales, and pipeline is useful for establishing trends, but telling teams they need to sell more stuff is like telling a race car driver they need to win more races. A more impactful way to optimize performance and drive accountability is to pair historical data with forward-looking metrics. Every Monday morning, I post the quarterly stack rank and results—a list of every seller, ranked by their quarterly attainment from high to low. If you are at the top of the list, you are generally happy. If you are at the bottom, hopefully you are motivated to move up. The intent is not to embarrass or taunt low performers but to show where people are trending against targets. Although these results are very recent, they are still historical and only tell half the story. By overlaying this historical data with forward-looking metrics, we can analyze trends, use the data to predict future outcomes, and tweak our approach.

One forward-looking metric I look at to drive a more predictable business is linearity. Linearity describes spreading out your bookings evenly over time rather than capturing them all at the end of a quarter or year. For example, let's say you are halfway or 50 percent through a fiscal quarter and last week's bookings brought your team to 25 percent of their quarterly revenue target. They would be behind the linearity target by 25 percent since 50 percent of the quarter has elapsed.[6] When sharing this data, I would coach the

---

6   In this example, 50 percent assumes standard seasonality. Seasonality refers to fluctuations in your sales forecast and revenue that are caused...

team on what is needed in the upcoming days, weeks, and months to ensure a more linear business. Perhaps we could incentivize earlier transactions and accelerate revenue by structuring our proposals to include time-bound financial incentives and limited time promotions.

Another forward-looking metric we use to drive predictable outcomes is pipeline creation. When I share last week's historical pipeline creation, I also talk about what is needed for future weeks, months, and quarters to stay ahead of the curve. For example, if a rep added $50,000 in new pipeline last week and you have set a weekly pipeline creation target of $250,000, they would need to add $450,000 this week to get back on track and make up for last week's $200,000 miss. Just telling a rep they need to add $450,000 this week isn't helpful; they need to understand what activities will impact their pipeline and where to spend time to maximize their efforts. This is why it is important to lay out clear targets and expectations when you acquire the team.

You can't hide behind numbers because numbers don't lie. There are other ways to hold teams accountable like attendance at events, participation in meetings, executive

---

...by external factors and occur on a predictable schedule around the same time(s) every year. In many cases, being halfway through a calendar quarter would not align to 50 percent linearity.

engagement, demand-generation activities, training and development, and so on, but numbers and metrics are the key to driving accountability and results.

Recognition

Recognition is one of the most powerful tools a sales leader possesses. It can be used not only to reward a high performer's effort, but also to send a message to those not recognized. Additionally, recognition can be used to demonstrate your appreciation and admiration for unsung heroes.

I once worked with a high-performing sales rep I'll call Tony. Tony won every top-seller award every quarter. He was always at the top of the stack rank, and his success seemed effortless. I watched people roll their eyes when Tony won the latest award while others who worked just as hard or harder went another quarter without any recognition. I couldn't change the rules just because I didn't like the outcome, so instead, I created a new award designed to recognize attributes beyond the numbers. I called this new award the SPF Award, which stood for Simplify, Performance, and Family.

- **Simplify:** Making everything easier; simplifying complex issues

- **Performance:** Going above and beyond in achievement, results, and goal attainment
- **Family:** Treating coworkers, partners, and customers with kindness, empathy, and respect

The SPF award was bestowed based on peer nominations, which made it even more meaningful. Every quarter I talked about the importance of the SPF award and emphasized the winner was selected by their peers. Tony continued to receive his top-seller awards but he never won the SPF award.

Some people loathe public recognition, and some people revel in it. Understanding individual motivations and desires is a critical factor when it comes to effective recognition. If deployed incorrectly, recognition can have an opposite than desired effect. You might think that publicly praising people will give them a morale boost, a pep in their step. But if public recognition makes them uncomfortable, they might try to stay off your radar to avoid future embarrassing experiences. Finding out how people like to be recognized is easy: just ask them, and they will tell you.

Consistency

As a leader you must do what you say you are going to do, and do it every time for everybody. If you do something for one, you must do it for all. Being consistent is not only the

ACQUIRE, BUILD, AND RUN

right thing to do, but it's the law in the United States to treat all employees equally.[7]

Being consistent means more than just treating people equally. Great leaders establish consistent business practices with widespread adoption to ensure that people are not left floundering or trying to invent their own methods.

A few years ago, my team was struggling with their forecast accuracy; some reps would commit a deal only to miss the predicted close date by weeks or months. A rep's ability to predict an exact date when a deal will close is a highly valued skill that most fail to master. I noticed that the reps who were consistently accurate with their sales forecasts shared some common behaviors and methods. To ensure that the best practices of the top performers were consistently adopted by the entire sales team, I instituted a weekly checkpoint call to review committed deals. I called it a checkpoint call because I checked off ten areas of risk that would cause a deal to slip from its forecasted close date. On these calls I would review the same ten points every week, leaving no stone unturned and ensuring every rep had access to the same consistent forecasting methods used by their peers. If the rep addressed all ten points

7   Be it enacted by the Senate and House of Representatives of the United States of America in Congress assembled, That this Act may be cited as the "Civil Rights Act of 1964."

satisfactorily, we would stick with the forecasted close date. If the rep failed to address all ten points, we would discuss the gaps, formulate a plan, revise the timeline, and update the committed close date.

The ten points we addressed on these calls were:

1. **Reverse Timeline:** Have you shared it with the customer and do they agree?
2. **Total Cost of Ownership:** Have you created and shared a TCO with the customer?
3. **Formal Proposal:** Have you presented the formal proposal to the customer?
4. **Executive Relationships:** Do we have relationships at the right levels?
5. **Order Process:** Do we know who needs to sign? Do they have budget and authority?
6. **Financial Incentives:** What will the customer lose if they don't do this deal?
7. **Value Proposition:** Does the customer see value in our solution?
8. **Competition:** Have we addressed all competitive objections?
9. **Technical Win:** Financials aside, are we the preferred technical solution?
10. **Have you asked for the order?**

People appreciate consistency, they find comfort in knowing what to expect. If you usually give out awards the first week of a new fiscal quarter, and then suddenly you don't, your team will be confused, disheartened, and unsettled.

Accountability, Recognition, and Consistency paired with the forty secrets from Chapter 5 is a recipe for smooth sailing as a sales leader. Getting your team to the point where they run with minimal intervention allows you the creative freedom to focus on your longer-term strategy and more audacious goals.

EIGHT

RECRUITING

f you want to guarantee your success as a sales leader, hire a great team. Manage underperformers out of your business, hire top sales reps, coach B players up to A players, set a high bar, and surround yourself with a team of like-minded, self-driven, accountable individuals who are the best at what they do. Recruiting top talent and surrounding yourself with people who are better than you allows you to spend more time on the strategic aspects of your business rather than dealing with inspection and performance management.

Sounds simple, right? It's not. In fact, assembling a team of rock stars is a massive undertaking that assumes you are the kind of leader people want to work for, you have a track record of success, you have fostered a culture of enablement, and you have already assembled a team of winners. Winners want to surround themselves with other winners, and it starts with you. Great leaders are always recruiting. Even if you don't have any immediate openings, if you find a great rep, you can keep them on your bench until the next spot opens up or refer them to a colleague at your company or even create a new role specifically targeted to that person's experience, expertise, relationships, or strengths.

As a leader, you are obligated to attract, retain, and develop the best talent you can find and ultimately identify your successor and the future leaders of the organization. Most companies have Human Resources and Talent Acquisition departments who assist in identifying and screening candidates, but you should be directly involved in the entire process from interviews to offers.

If you interview five people for a job and select one person, that means that there are four people who didn't get the job and have formed an opinion about you, the way you operate, your hiring process, and your company. Those four people might go on to work for your customers, partners, or competitors, so running a straightforward and transparent hiring process is vital.

Interviewing is a lot of work when done properly, but most people do not do it properly. When bringing candidates into the office for multiple interviews, I hand them gift bags labeled "Interview Survival Kit." Each contains a bottle of water, a snack, a coffee mug, some gum, and hand sanitizer, all emblazoned with my company's logo. It's a small gesture that goes a long way in putting people at ease and showing them you care.

Never subject your candidates to more than four separate interviews for a sales rep role, and ideally, complete the four interviews within one or two days. Keep in mind that your candidates are taking time out of their days, often while working other jobs, to go through your hiring process. I've heard about some processes that drag on for months. That's crazy!

Choose your interview panel carefully so that it represents a cross-section of your company with diversity in thought and responsibility. Each interviewer should have a clear understanding of the traits you are looking for and a bank of questions to choose from that you have prepared. In a recent search for a first line leader, I sent the interview panel this list of potential questions:

Some potential questions to ask external candidates:
- Why do you want this? Why here? Why now?
- What do people come to you for?
- What do you think your brand is?
- What is your proudest career moment?

- What is your experience with subscription sales and as-a-service offerings?
- What is your experience with large, complex, strategic pursuits?
- What is your channel philosophy?
- What is your leadership philosophy?
- What will be your day-one messaging to the team?
- Where do you anticipate spending time during your first thirty days (percentage)—internal, customer, partner?
- How will you handle underperforming reps?
- What concerns, roadblocks, or pitfalls do you anticipate?
- How much do you know about our company? Recent earnings, portfolio, market position, share, competition, etc.
- What does a great culture look like to you?
- How do you structure your days/weeks/months?
- How do you track your team's activity?
- What do you think the role of a sales leader is?
- How do you utilize your engineering counterparts in your business? What role do they play?

Some potential questions to ask internal candidates:
- Why do you want to be a sales leader?

- What would you *start* doing that the previous sales leader was not doing?
- What would you *stop* doing that the previous sales leader was doing?
- What would you *continue* doing that the previous sales leader was doing?
- What do you think is holding the team back from better performance?
- What would you do differently to drive revenue within this district?
- Stack rank the team (A players, B players, C players). What is your plan for each?
- What is your day-one messaging to the team?
- Who is the first person you call if you get the job?
- How would you feel if you don't get the job?
- What is your messaging to your peers who applied but did not get the job?
- Would you consider yourself process-driven or results-driven?
- In what ways have you demonstrated leadership in your current role?
- Provide five cross-segment leadership references outside of your current team.
- How have you handled conflicts, revenue splits, etc.?

- Have you been through our internal leadership
  training program? If not, have you applied or been
  nominated?

When all of the interviews are complete, ask your interviewers to email you their rankings (best to worst). After you have assembled all the rankings in writing, schedule a group discussion with the interview panel. In a group setting, the group tends to reach the same conclusion to avoid friction and conflict, a phenomenon known as groupthink. This is why gathering feedback in writing before meeting as a group is important. In the meeting, ask the interviewers, in order of seniority from low to high (to avoid influence), to share the experiences they had with each candidate and provide some additional context behind their rankings.

Once you have reached a decision and informed the candidates, provide feedback and coaching to those who did not get the job. These people will form an opinion about you and your team based on this limited interaction, and they will take their opinions with them when they leave. Your responsibility as the leader is to ensure the company's reputation and brand is still intact when the dust settles.

NINE

LEADING LEADERS

Sales leaders are people too. Just like sales reps, leaders have varying motivations, personalities, and styles. People who have chosen and been selected for leadership roles see something in themselves that sets them apart from the pack. They might not yet fully believe in their abilities or have a fully formed leadership style, but they hear that internal voice saying, "If not me, then who?" But they can't do it alone. Leaders need leaders too.

Just as there are different levels of sales representatives, there are different levels of sales leaders. In sales, the reps are often referred to as the front line, their direct sales manager as a first line leader, the sales manager's manager as a second line leader, and so on up the chain. As a second line (or higher) leader, you have the interesting and challenging task of leading multiple sales leaders, who in turn lead their own sales teams. There are some parallels between leading sales reps and leading sales leaders, but for the most part, leading leaders requires an entirely different approach.

Leadership is not for everybody. The handful of us who felt obligated to step away from the group and embark on a leadership journey seek inspiration and wisdom from those who have been down the same road. Many times we feel like we are in over our heads, like we don't belong in the role, as if we tricked people into thinking we are qualified for a job we actually have no business doing. This feeling of being a fraud is known as imposter syndrome, a common feeling shared by high achievers who find it hard to accept their triumphs.

Leaders want to be acknowledged. They need reassurance that they belong in the role and possess the necessary qualities and traits to be successful. They thrive when they feel recognized, empowered, and enabled to fully utilize their creative differentiators. As their leader, you must unleash their full potential and work toward achieving an operating level of high trust, enablement, and independence.

New leaders are eager to prove themselves and they are learning quickly. If there are bad processes in place, they learn them quickly. If there are good processes in place, they learn them quickly. Your job is to lay out a path to success made up of good processes (activity, coaching, hiring, and so on). Things that are well known and understood should be shared and discussed regularly to shorten their path to success and avoid reinventing the wheel.

As a second line leader, sometimes you will find yourself serving as a mediator. When issues can't be resolved on the front lines, first line leaders might bring the issues to you for resolution. For example, because sales teams are often in dispersed geographical locations, they might compete with each other and fight over turf. The higher you rise in an organization, the more important being a decisive leader who takes action without waffling, wavering, or flip-flopping is. Your goal should be to resolve all issues at your level—make sure the buck stops with you. People are hungry for decisive leadership; they want the conflict resolved and to put it behind them. If the decision is outside of their control, they will be satisfied, even if it does not go their way.

Sometimes the solution to a problem on the front line that seems glaringly obvious to you as a second line leader is not as obvious to your first line leaders because they are too close to the issue. Let's use the example of "Richard," one of your sales reps who reports to first line leader "Amy"

(Fig. 6) and is having performance issues. Richard is measured on his attainment against a revenue goal and his bookings. Since his bookings are below expected targets, you look for an issue with his pipeline; a robust pipeline is a good indicator of future bookings, and ideally, sales reps are always actively building new pipeline while simultaneously closing existing pipeline. You find that Richard's pipeline is insufficient, so you check his activity. You discover his activity is insufficient to create a pipeline, which means a larger underlying issue probably needs to be addressed. (There's an adage in sales worth remembering: activity leads to pipeline, and pipeline leads to bookings.)

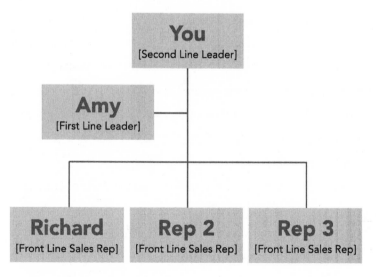

Fig. 6. Richard & Amy's org chart.

You now have to determine: Is Richard motivated? Is he dealing with a personal issue? Has he had sufficient product training and enablement? Has his manager been coaching and guiding him? Should he be placed on a performance improvement plan (PIP)?[8]

Part of being a leader is trusting your gut when it comes to people. Impactful decisions like hiring, firing, and promoting require you to be a good judge of character. Perhaps you saw Richard present a solution to a customer, and as a result, you have no confidence in his ability to improve. Maybe you heard him bragging about his new car and question his self-awareness. The question becomes how you, as a second line leader, should address the Richard problem given that Amy, not you, is Richard's direct manager.

Whether you hired Amy or inherited her, she is a leader on your team and your job is to enable her independence and help guide her toward a decision. But you can't make decisions for her. If you believe Richard's performance needs to be formally addressed and Amy isn't taking sufficient action, first ask her how she believes Richard is doing. She likely will agree that his performance is not

---

8   A PIP lays out criteria for improvement, including key milestones and
    metrics that must be achieved within a certain timeframe to avoid
    termination. Issuing a PIP is usually a last resort and often ends in
    termination. The appropriate duration of a PIP is debatable, but I suggest
    forty-five days is sufficient for most reps to demonstrate success or failure.

at the level required, because numbers don't lie, but she might have additional information that you can't see at your level. The conversation typically will go one of three ways from there:

1. Amy is aware of Richard's performance issues. She is in the early stages of digging into the fundamentals of his business to understand where he is facing challenges. She is going to report back with findings and seek your guidance on a coaching plan for Richard.

2. Amy is aware of Richard's performance issues. She has dug into his business and discovered (for example) that his assigned vertical was recently impacted by cost reductions outside of his control. He is doing all the right things but not seeing the results due to macroeconomic issues. She is concerned that Richard might get frustrated and that he is a "flight risk." If Richard has been a valued contributor historically and has a track record of satisfactory performance, you might encourage Amy to align Richard to a new vertical or account list to see if his performance improves. You also might offer

Richard a financial retention incentive to avoid losing him to a competitor.

3. Amy is aware of Richard's performance issues, but she seems to be excusing him. She says things like, "It's hard to get meetings in his area" and "The competition has been fierce in his accounts." In situations like this, you need to determine if Amy's observations are legitimate or just excuses. At this point, scheduling a "skip level" meeting with Richard to form your own opinion is appropriate, after which you will report back to Amy with a recommended get-well plan. In your skip level meeting, stick to metrics and facts, clearly articulate what is expected, identify where Richard is falling short, and provide coaching. Afterward, document everything you discussed in an email to Richard. Most companies require a documented history of performance and coaching prior to separating with an employee to legally limit their liability should a disgruntled employee choose to sue for wrongful termination.

Here's an example of the recap email I would send to Richard following his performance-focused skip level meeting:

Richard,

Thank you for taking some time to review your performance with me today. Per our discussion, significant performance improvement is required in your territory.

The primary metrics we use to evaluate performance are: Bookings and Attainment, Pipeline, and Activity.

Bookings and Attainment:
Your lifetime bookings are approximately $1 million, which is not sufficient to sustain your patch. You have not yet achieved a quarterly or annual goal in your time at this company (performance history attached to email).

Pipeline:
Your current Q1 advanced stage pipeline is $190,000. Based on your Q1 quota of $727,000 and 60 percent historical close rates and a 3X pipeline target, your advanced stage pipeline should be at least $2.2 million. You currently have a Q1 advanced stage pipeline deficit of $2 million.

Activity:
The activity required to develop pipeline (and ultimately bookings) should include daily customer and partner-facing meetings, demand-generation campaigns

in conjunction with marketing, localized or web-based events, whitespace mapping, executive engagement sessions, ecosystem interaction, and internal strategy sessions. How you structure your days and weeks is an important part of driving activity. Based on your shared calendar (screenshots attached to email), you are not currently driving enough activity to generate pipeline in your patch. We are a numbers- and metrics-driven organization. We are all held accountable to delivering revenue to the business, and your success is an important part of the success of the region. Your manager will follow up with you directly regarding this conversation.

Thank you,
Adam

This email might seem harsh or cold—this is by design. I intentionally focus on only facts and metrics. The wording in this email is carefully chosen such that I would feel comfortable having it presented in a courtroom deposition on a large display in front of a jury (although I'm not a lawyer, so seek your own legal advice). In the opening paragraph, I use a pleasant and grateful tone (*Thank you for taking some time to review your performance with me today*). I am not hostile toward this individual. I also use the first paragraph to clearly articulate the issue that was discussed (*performance improvement is required in your territory*).

I go on to explain how performance is measured, leaving no room for interpretation (*The primary metrics we use to evaluate performance are: Bookings and Attainment, Pipeline, and Activity*) and provide specific, actionable coaching and guidance that demonstrates our ongoing commitment to his success (*daily customer and partner-facing meetings, demand generation campaigns in conjunction with marketing,...*).

In this case, let's say you learned that Amy is too close to Richard. They have become friends outside of work, their kids go to the same school, they are hanging out on weekends, and as a result, Amy is protecting Richard's lack of performance. If Amy is unable to effectively lead her team because she has created an "us versus you" mindset, then you need to do Amy's job for her in the short term and provide her with direct and actionable coaching. You need to get Amy to a place of high trust, where you can lead the sales reps *through* her and help her draw her own conclusions, form her own opinions, and reach your shared objective in her own way.

As leaders, we sometimes think that our way of doing things is the best way just because our way produced results in the past. Oftentimes people can achieve the same or greater results by taking a different approach than yours. I always tell my teams, "You don't have to do it my way; in fact, I would prefer you do things in your own authentic way that you feel passionately about, as long as you achieve the same or better end result."

Second line leaders often experience a magical moment when everything clicks. The plane is at cruising altitude, everyone is swimming in the same direction, and things just feel right. It's that feeling you get when you are outpacing the business, when you are ahead of the curve and you have unlocked a time portal to resupply, reload, and accelerate growth. You will know when you achieve this special moment because everything becomes crystal clear, as if a bright blue light is guiding you through a dark forest. Forks in the road become obvious choices, and leading your team through the woods to green pastures is a certainty. When you reach this phase as a leader, the best thing you can do for your team is try and stay out of their way, remove obstacles, and let them fly...all while making preparations behind the scenes for the next dark forest they might encounter.

TEN

COMMUNICATION

My first marriage ended in divorce. A lot of marriages end in divorce. The reasons are numerous and complicated. If you ask most people what caused the breakdown of their marriage, they will likely offer up lists of complaints about their ex-partners. In hindsight, all of the issues in my own marriage boiled down to a communication failure. Plenty of words were exchanged, but we couldn't seem to understand each other's viewpoint. What I didn't realize at the time is that my ex-wife and I have very different and opposing communication styles.

Countless studies have been done around the ways people communicate, and the conclusions drawn are all similar. Effectively, each of us communicates in the style that works best for our personalities—the style that best processes information and feels natural and comfortable to us. Your preferred communication style is shaped by your surroundings and environment. If you were raised in a household where children should be seen and not heard, you might be hesitant to voice your opinion. If you were one of six siblings, you might be more vocal or inclined to speak up in group settings in order to make your voice heard. Regardless of how people acquire their communication styles, everybody has one. Your communication style determines the way in which you prefer to send, receive, and process information.

Communication styles, for the most part, can be categorized into four primary style groups (Fig. 7). First, there are the people who like to use a lot of details and a lot of words. Let's call this the Wordy group. Second are those who value brevity and simplicity, often glossing over details to get straight to the point. Let's call this the Shorty group. Third, we have the dominant, aggressive types who make decisions quickly, focus on results, are viewed as intense, and are often comfortable being the loudest voice in a room. Let's call this the Aggro group. Finally, there is the fourth group, people who are social, outgoing, enthusiastic, full of energy, and fun to be around, but might be viewed as a little emotional at times and lacking concrete facts. Let's call this the Party group.

You probably find yourself leaning toward one group already, likely because it feels the most natural to you. Keep in mind, you might not fit perfectly into one group; you might straddle two. Let's delve into these groups a little further.

Wordy

If you are in the Wordy group, you cannot straddle the Shorty group; they are opposites. Wordys have the hardest time communicating with Shortys. Wordys love to provide lots of details and supporting information and might even speak tangentially. This kind of communication style is frustrating for the Shorty, who can't follow along and just wants the Wordy to get to the point. Wordys can, however, straddle the Party group. In fact, most people in the Party group are also Wordys.

Shorty

Shortys can seem cold and calculated at times, without intending to. Shortys love using the fewest words possible to convey a message. They might reply to emails with a single word or boil a very complicated issue down to a few sentences. Those higher up in an organization often exhibit this kind of communication. Executives with limited time and hundreds of tasks use brevity as a means to resolve a task and move to the next. There is a reason they require executive *summaries* and *briefs*; executives don't have time for long-winded explanations and lots of details. The ability to communicate complicated issues in a simple, boiled-down manner is a highly valued leadership trait. The downside to being a Shorty is you might overlook details or leave out important facts. By lacking a process-driven, analytical perspective and driving straight to the finish line, you can miss opportunities along the way. Shortys have the hardest time communicating with Wordys, but Shortys love talking to other Shortys, and some find they are also in the Aggro group.

Aggro

Aggros are close cousins of Shortys but with one exception: they are more aggressive than Shortys. While a Shorty can be shy, an Aggro is never shy. Aggros are dominant, loud, fast-talking, and sometimes viewed as overbearing. An Aggro has no problem communicating with a Shorty as long as the Shorty lets the Aggro be the loudest voice in the room. However, Aggros cannot straddle the Wordy group.

Party

The Party group is the fun group! If you are a Party, you are likely most comfortable around friends in a social setting, telling stories and laughing about good times. You might be emotional and sensitive, talk about how things make you feel, and use a lot of words to convey your point. Partys can easily communicate with Wordys, but they have a hard time with Shortys and Aggros.

♦ To the point
♦ Not a lot of details
♦ Concise
♦ Closest to Aggro
♦ Opposite of Wordy

♦ Dominant
♦ Aggressive
♦ Loud
♦ Closest to Shorty
♦ Opposite of Party

Shorty

Aggro

Party

Wordy

♦ Outgoing
♦ Friendly
♦ Emotional
♦ Closest to Wordy
♦ Opposite of Aggro

♦ Lots of details
♦ Analytical
♦ Goes on tangents
♦ Closest to Party
♦ Opposite of Shorty

Fig. 7. Communication styles.

It would be nice if everyone had tattoos on their forehead that identified their communication styles, but ultimately, it's up to you to observe and determine the way people prefer to communicate. As a leader, knowing your own communication style and that of your team is critical for effective communication. Once you have identified your communication group(s), think about a time you had a conflict or struggle with somebody where you just couldn't see eye to eye. This person likely has a communication style that is diametrically opposed to yours (Wordy vs. Shorty or Party vs. Aggro), and neither of you were willing to flex toward the middle.

Once you are aware of your communication style, you can use a couple of techniques to work on flexing to embrace other people's preferred communication methods, which eases tension and creates opportunities to enlighten yourself with a new perspective. The simplest technique is called mirroring—observing somebody's pace, pattern, and tone of speech and matching it. For example, I once did business with a guy I'll call Mitch who spoke like he was stuck on fast-forward. He was obviously in the Aggro group. Whenever I spoke with Mitch, I let him speak first because I know Aggros like that. I increased the speed of my speech and always let him have the last word. People struggled to work with and communicate with Mitch. He had a reputation for being a self-centered, aggressive fast-talker. Although I am a Shorty, Mitch and I never had issues communicating because I knew how to flex toward his style and mirror his pace.

As a sales leader and self-proclaimed Shorty, I sometimes struggled to communicate with the Wordy members of my team. I found myself losing the point of conversations and asking them to slow down, re-explain, and summarize, just so I could follow along. Conversely, they were equally frustrated by my lack of detail and inability to understand their points. When opposite groups like Shortys and Wordys try to communicate, being up front and explicit about communication differences helps both sides work toward accommodating each other. I once had a rep on my team who was an extreme Wordy, so I asked him to please exclude some supporting information and try to get to the point faster, and I promised that in exchange I would do my best to provide more detailed, analytical, and actionable feedback, the way he preferred.

Identifying people's communication styles can take some practice. Make a list of people you interact with every day: your spouse, children, parents, coworkers, and others. Try to determine their communication groups, and the next time you communicate with them, attempt to match their styles as best as possible. As you flex toward their styles, you likely will notice more engagement and acknowledgment compared to prior conversations with that person.

Ideally, you should strive to create a form of communication between you and your team that transcends the basic styles of verbal interaction. The ideal state of communication between leaders and their teams exists when operating under such high conditions of trust, empowerment, and enablement that decisions are made and actions are taken without the need for preemptive communication. Nonverbal, mutual agreement without the fear of recourse creates velocity in business that would otherwise not exist. Before you can achieve this rare utopian state of nonverbal communication, you must set clear expectations, communicate explicitly, and leave no room for interpretation.

As a leader, your communication must be explicit, honest, direct, concise, transparent, authentic, and deliberate. You cannot be a great leader if you are not a great communicator. Carefully chosen words are especially important during difficult conversations, such as when delivering bad news.

As a leader, your words carry weight and have repercussions. Those repercussions could be legal or financial (wrongful termination, harassment, discrimination, etc.) in some cases.

As a leader, you should have limited, impactful, and intentional touch points with your team. If you over-communicate, your voice will become "noise" and your message will be lost. If you under-communicate, your message won't be found. Not only do you need to manage your own communication style, but you should also be aware of others'. You can't control the actions of your peers or superiors, but if somebody is barraging your team with too much communication, your job is to shield them from unnecessary distractions and keep them focused on their mission.

Striking the right tone is an often overlooked component of effective communication. Saying "I really need you to take care of this" with a smile and a pat on the back is a lot different than saying "I *really* need you to take care of this!" in a stern, loud voice. Conveying tone in written communication is especially difficult, so being explicit and intentional becomes even more important to avoid your message getting misconstrued.

Your tone can evolve over time. For example, in Chapter 7 I recommended using a more aggressive tone when first acquiring a team and softening up later. You might have noticed this book starts with a more formal tone, citing research and facts, but becomes more casual once we've "gotten to know each other." Over time, as coworkers become familiar with each other, their tone becomes more conversational and informal, like two friends catching up over lunch. As a leader, you can use tone to garner trust and add emphasis to your message.

Intentional and thoughtful communication can change people's lives. The most meaningful conversations I've had with great leaders reverberated in my brain, haunting me until I took action. A leader once asked me, "Where do you want to be, and what are you waiting for?"

Great leaders use their words to inspire action.

ELEVEN

CONCLUSION

D o you have washboard abs and a perfect physique? If you're a late-night snacker who can't say no to peanut butter cups like me, you probably gave up on having a chiseled torso at some point in your twenties. Having a vision of my ideal body, making a plan to get there, and taking action toward that goal would still prove to be an impossible feat for me because I just don't care enough about it to put in the required work. I would rather spend my free time with family or hobbies than living in a gym and counting macros.

If we want something badly enough, we will figure out a way to make it happen, and if we don't, we won't. Let's imagine for a moment that someone told me, "I will give you $10 million if you can get washboard abs within the next twelve months." I would drop everything and get to work. I would start by cementing my vision; my walls would be covered with posters of my current doughy abdomen next to chiseled torsos for comparison and inspiration. Next, I would assemble a team to coauthor a plan for success. I would hire a medical doctor, nutritionist, personal trainer, private chef, yoga instructor, and maybe even a therapist. Assembling a large team of professionals to help me achieve my goal would be a relatively small up-front investment considering the reward. Plus, a lofty goal such as this requires a group effort where everybody is aligned and focused on a singular objective; I wouldn't be able to do it alone.

Once everything was in place, I would get to work eating clean, lifting weights, running, and doing sit-ups until I puked. I have zero doubt that the outcome of this effort would be washboard abs and a $10 million payday.

Unfortunately, nobody is paying me to get in shape so I'll have to live with my dad bod for now. The obvious point here is that if you want something badly enough, you will figure out how to make it a reality—and $10 million can buy a lot of peanut butter cups.

If you are struggling to achieve a goal, try tweaking the motivation. Keeping the goal the same but simply changing the motivation has an amazing effect; you are propelled toward action. The reason most people don't take action in the direction of their goal is that they just don't want it badly enough.

In the introduction of this book, I challenged the notion that only 10 percent of people can lead, and I shared my belief that anybody can be an effective sales leader. I hope you now understand what I mean by that. Anyone can be an effective sales leader *if they want it badly enough to put in the work.* When you conduct a thorough self-examination, identify your true motivations, set a vision, create a plan, and take action, you truly can achieve anything.

Hoping everything will fall into place without a plan is a plan to fail. You have agency over your life; establish a plan to reach your goals and take meaningful steps every day toward realizing your grandest visions. If that sounds scary to you, don't worry; it should. Achieving big things requires big, uncomfortable, consistent actions. Most people shy away from discomfort, but if you've made it this far in the book, you're not like most people.

Leadership is a challenging path fraught with pitfalls, resistance, and obstacles. Some people will relent and blend back into the crowd, and others will embrace the challenge and go on to be great leaders. Unfortunately, some people will ignore the advice in this book and become shitty leaders. Don't worry about those people. Be a great coach for your team, be a great parent to your children, be a great partner to your spouse, and focus on what you can control. Shitty leaders will always exist, but you aren't one of them.

What you do with the information in this book is entirely up to you. From my experience, everyone can be divided into one of two groups, people who *do* and people who *don't*. The "doers" are people who take action in every aspect of their lives. They see trash on the street and pick it up. They return shopping carts to the corral at the supermarket. They can't walk past a full dishwasher without emptying it. They take big swings and they make things happen. The doers are self-aware. They understand that it will take a lot of work to achieve great outcomes, and they flourish when they surround themselves with like-minded, driven individuals who also are prepared to put in the work.

The "don't" group is comfortable being comfortable. They are satisfied with the status quo. They procrastinate and put off until tomorrow the things that could be done today. They know what they *should* do ("I should work out, I should get in shape, I should call my mother..."), but they don't. If you find yourself in this group, don't worry, you are not relegated to this group forever unless you want to be. You still can achieve great things but you are going to have to work a little harder, fight your natural instincts, and force yourself to take action. Turn your *shoulds* into *musts* and great things will follow: "I *must* call my mother, I *must* get in shape, I *must* take the necessary steps to become a great leader."

The world needs great leaders. When you look back on your career, you won't remember the deals, the sales, the wins, the issues. You will remember the people you touched, the lives you impacted, the difference you made. If you can't make a list of one hundred people you have personally helped, then keep helping until you can. If you can easily list one hundred people, then add a zero and strive for a thousand! Go make a huge impact!

What do you want to be known for? What is a word that you hope people will use to describe you? What kind of leader do you want to be? Where are you going and how will you get there? What is your wildest dream?

The key to achieving your wildest dreams is you. Nobody is going to do this for you. Don't wait for permission. Don't wait for a sign. Just start today. If it was easy, everybody would do it. What are you waiting for?

Thank you for taking the time to invest in yourself and your team. Continue the conversation at AdamApps.com and on social media using the hashtag #ShittySalesLeaders.

ACKNOWLEDGMENTS

For my wife, **Meredith,** thank you for your relentless encouragement and unwavering support. We have accomplished so much together and none of it would be possible without you. Even this book wouldn't exist without your encouragement (and edits). You keep our lives on track and keep us moving forward. I am so lucky to have you in my life; I can't wait to write our next chapter together. I love you!

For my son, **Adam George,** you are my life. Your kindness, passion, and excitement inspire me to be a better person. You've had the unfortunate experience of being a sounding board for my motivational speeches and daily life lessons, but you're a very generous listener and an amazing human. Thank you for your input on this book; you are wise beyond your years and I appreciate your insights on natural selection! Your gentle soul makes this world a brighter place. Manifest your wildest dreams; I love you!

For my parents, **Sue** and **Dave,** and my sister, **Gemma.** We have been through so much over the last few decades; we've moved across oceans, faced challenges, enjoyed triumphs, experienced losses, and welcomed new family members. Whatever we faced, we faced it together, and I am blessed to call you my family. Thank you for your ever-lasting and unconditional support. I love you!

For my best friend, best man, and godfather to my son, **Peter Cooper.** You are one of the kindest people I know. Your calm approach has influenced me in more ways than you know. You have stuck with me through all my shenanigans and I'm so grateful for all of our shared life experiences. Thank you for always being a steady, reliable, caring extension of my family. Love you, man!

This book is also dedicated to the great leaders with whom I have had the privilege of working. Some leaders might be surprised to see their names acknowledged below, but their impact was deeper and more meaningful than they probably realize.

Thank you, **Dave "Hat" Hatfield,** you are not just somebody who generously agreed to write the foreword to this book, you are my touchstone leader. You just "get it." In our time working together, I saw you show an entire company how a great leader can be kind, authentic, vulnerable, fearless, inspirational, and incredibly effective. When I'm faced with a challenging situation, I ask myself, "What would Hat do?" You set a high bar and inspire me to do more every day. You are the hypothetical great leader referenced throughout this book and have touched the lives of countless people who have had the privilege of working with you. Thank you for the massive impact you've made!

Thank you, **Lou DeMarco**, for hiring a young punk with no experience right out of college. All I had to offer you was my work ethic and my word; you were willing to give a stranger a shot, and for that I am eternally grateful. You showed me how a compassionate leader can make a team feel like family and an office feel like home. You gave me suits; you gave me advice; and you gave me my start. Thank you.

Thank you, **Jesse Childs**, you taught me so much about what it takes to build a business. Your best practices, lessons, and leadership stuck with me throughout my career. You are a genuine, authentic, thoughtful leader who gets shit done.

Thank you, **Mike O'Grady**, you hired me into one of the largest tech companies in the world and lovingly threw me into the deep end of the pool. You trusted in my abilities and took me under your wing. You were so much more than a great leader; you were my mentor, financial advisor, voice of reason, and friend.

Thank you, **Mark Niemiec**, you gave me the gift of feedback and taught me how to take control of my brand and my career. You taught me how to manage up and have tough conversations. You showed me the importance of consistency and recognition. I have always carried your lessons with me.

Thank you, **Bill Kohut**, you gave me my first real leadership role. You had plenty of qualified candidates, but you saw something in me and put me on a path that would change the course of my career (and life) forever. Your own leadership journey has been inspirational to watch, and I am grateful for your guidance and friendship. I look forward to retiring in New England and visiting often!

Thank you, **Pete Agresta**, you showed me what true empowerment looks like. I have never felt more enabled, entrusted, and inspired than I did during my time working with you. You gave me a platform and a stage (literally) to be my true, authentic self. At times, you believed in me more than I believed in myself, and you understood a side of me that most people did not. You showed me what it meant to lead a business through leaders, and you promoted me into a position you knew would ruffle some feathers. You are fearless; you live and breathe ownership and accountability every single day. You work harder than most people I know, and somehow you still find time for everyone. I am so grateful for our time working together, and I credit you with a significant growth spurt in my leadership journey and for giving me the push I needed to finish this book. Thank you for your trust, friendship, and generously improvised guitar solos.

Thank you, **Kevin Delane**, you are the definition of an inspirational leader. You are one of the most beloved sales leaders I have ever known, and you have a natural talent for motivation. You put me on stage in front of thousands of people and gave me opportunities to thrive. I will never forget the battles we fought and the wins we shared. You are a true salesperson's leader and one of a kind. EFD!

Thank you, **Charles Giancarlo.** You may call yourself a workhorse (and not a show pony), but your fearless leadership and willingness to dive in and show up has inspired thousands. I knew when you flew across the country, overnight, during a nor'easter to meet with clients in New York, you were a different kind of CEO. It would be easy (and expected) for a CEO to be inaccessible, unapproachable, or arrogant, but instead you are kind, thoughtful, and authentic. You are a humble servant who genuinely cares about his organization, and you use your platform to advance meaningful and important causes. You are living proof that it is possible to drive incredible results, make difficult decisions, and transform an industry, all while being a great human. Thank you for showing me a side of a CEO that I didn't know could exist. I am honored and filled with pride to say I was part of your team. Thank you for your insights on forward-looking metrics and accountability and thank you for setting such a high bar and being one of the great leaders who inspired this book.

Thank you, **Dan Fitzsimmons,** for being so generous with your time. Even after a well-deserved promotion to Global CRO, you kept our biweekly call on the calendar and always took the time to listen and provide guidance. You embody authentic and sincere leadership, and I consider myself one of the fortunate people who has had the opportunity to work with you. Thank you for always having my back, trusting me to make big decisions, and providing inspirational leadership. I owe you drinks at Cloud Nine!

Thank you, **Andy Martin,** for showing me what authentic leadership looks like. Your direct, honest, and thoughtful approach inspires confidence and trust. You light up a room and put a smile on people's faces, all while holding people accountable and driving results. I have learned so much from you about navigating a career in leadership, simply by doing the right thing, being honest, and trusting your gut. You make it look effortless. I appreciate your leadership, friendship, and financial advice. See you on the beach in twenty years!

Thank you, **Matt Burr,** for generously mentoring me through the early days of my second line leadership journey and by unknowingly serving as my aspirational goalpost. I learned so much from my time working with you, and I can't wait for the right opportunity to hire a mariachi band to accompany me to a party.

Thank you, **Joe Gutowski,** for serving as a voice of reason, a model of calm, and a sounding board. I've learned a ton from your approach and appreciate your guidance, support, and leadership throughout my journey.

Thank you, **Brent Allen,** for having the guts to walk away from an established role at a reputable company and paving the way to greener pastures. You showed me that success should not be the consolation prize for tolerating a toxic work environment and that it is possible to be successful, supported, empowered, and happy all at the same time!

Thank you, **Agan Singh,** for meeting me at a bar in midtown Manhattan early in my career and teaching me the importance of knowing yourself and your story before embarking on a leadership journey.

Thank you, **Lynne Doherty,** for your mentorship and wisdom. You always made sure I knew my "buts" and was "brilliant in the basics." Your best practices have served as a mental playbook throughout my career.

Thank you, **Joe Waleck**, for being a great friend and business partner. You set a high bar for effective leadership and have kept me smiling throughout the years. It's rare to have someone to bounce ideas off who really understands the plight. Thanks for being such a great human!

The list of people who have shaped my journey is endless. To everyone who has been in the trenches with me along the way, put up with my crazy ideas, provided support, and offered advice—thank you for making a positive impact!

APPENDIX A

ARTICLES

About once a year I gather my thoughts on leadership and publicly share some lessons from my ongoing leadership journey. I posted the following articles on social media platforms. They served as a public diary for all the world to see, open to scrutiny, criticism, and comments. Knowing I might look back in a few years with a different perspective, I wanted to ensure these milestones were captured at those particular moments in time. I've collected a few of my articles here.

5 MISTAKES I MADE AS A NEW MANAGER (AND HOW TO AVOID THEM)

Originally published February 26, 2017, on LinkedIn.com

As I approach the anniversary of my entry into management, or formal leadership, it feels like a good time to take pause, put pen to paper, or fingers to keyboard, and reflect upon some things I've done well and not so well over the past 12 months; hopefully others find something useful here to shorten their leadership ramp.

When I made the transition from Individual Contributor to Regional Manager, I quickly found out the realities of the job are quite different from the outside looking in. For the past decade I had been insulated from the realities of the leadership role by the great leaders of my past; in short, they made a nearly insurmountable task seem effortless.

Much like becoming a new parent, a new leader is no longer only responsible for him or herself; instead, the decisions you make have far reaching implications including people's livelihoods and families. Your success as a leader is contingent upon your ability to execute quickly and effectively while inspiring a group of people towards a common goal—all while working within the confines of your organization; this effort is hindered only by your lack of experience or a handful of well-intended missteps.

I could've easily written an article entitled "50 Mistakes I Made As a New Manager." I decided instead to focus my attention on five major areas that could shorten a new leader's ramp up time and have the greatest impact on their team.

1. Stick to Your Plan: Almost everybody entering a new role will have a well-crafted 30-60-90-day business plan. If you've done your homework, spoken with people in the role and spent some time collecting your ideas, it's not difficult to create a solid, well-structured plan of attack; the hard part is sticking to it.

In the first few months as a new leader, you will be pulled in a million directions. People will want time on your calendar, clients and business partners will want issues addressed quickly, you will likely have a new direct manager, new tools to learn, inherited problems, conflicts to resolve, new processes, new contacts, new expectations and an entirely new team with unique personalities and motivations. It would be very easy to stray from your original plan and modify it to match your current situation; It's definitely ok to flex and modify your strategy on the fly, but it's critical that you use your original plan as a to-do list. If they were good ideas before you started, back in the simple days when you still had a clear head, they are more than likely still good ideas that should be executed.

2. Start Strong: Probably the best advice I received before I started in my new role was "Come out of the gate strong, you can soften up later; it's nearly impossible to start soft and toughen up later." I've heard similar advice for people headed to prison; not sure what that says about management.

As an individual contributor, I always appreciated a strong leader with a rigid structure and well-defined requirements. I knew where I stood and I knew exactly what was expected from me.

3. Address Issues Quickly: You rarely hear someone say, "I wish I waited longer to take action." You likely have a good sense of where the issues are before you start in the role, and you were hired for a reason, to address them quickly and move on. Assuming you know where the problems are, don't wait around for them to fix themselves. They will inevitably get worse.

4. Just Say "No": As a new leader, a lot will be asked of you: early mornings, late nights, days full of meetings and new commitments. I said "yes" to every request that crossed my desk in the first few months but it was to the detriment of critical areas of our business that were less noisy. Sometimes the squeaky wheel shouldn't get the oil; it should get a "no." It took almost nine months for me to realize that it is ok to decline, postpone or delegate some requests. There are only so many hours in the day and they need to be allocated efficiently.

5. Know Your Role: Probably my biggest mistake was falling back into my old role as Account Manager, trying to lead strategy, run meetings, drive revenue and set agendas. That behavior undermines the role of the Account Manager and blurs the line between individual and leader. It's important to remind yourself to "listen twice as much as you speak" and ask yourself "is what I'm about to do or say helping this person to be successful?" Luckily, I caught this mistake early and corrected myself, but I've seen people fall back into this trap because there is a fine line between being helpful and taking over.

To simplify my lessons learned: it's important to understand that as a manager, you have an opportunity to be the best boss someone has ever had; don't take it lightly and work hard every day to be the kind of leader you would run through walls for.

TIME KILLS ALL DEALS? NOT SO FAST...

Originally published January 29, 2018, on LinkedIn.com

If you're in sales you've likely heard the adage, "Time Kills All Deals." I was a firm believer in this sentiment for many years, until recently.

If you break down the statement "time kills all deals," we are really talking about the potential for unknown variables to enter a sales cycle, inject uncertainty and create entry points for your competition; at best delaying your sale and at worst jeopardizing the entire transaction.

What if we rethink the entire paradigm of time as it relates to the sales cycle and instead think of time as an instrument to remove uncertainty, garner trust and accumulate additional buy-in from key stakeholders and grow your deal?

I'm not suggesting you intentionally elongate a sales cycle (a bird in hand, etc.), but there are occasions when taking a step back and allowing a sale to progress organically can be beneficial for a few reasons:

1. Trust: Sales reps already know that coming across as 'pushy' or 'desperate' to a buyer only serves to reduce the trust and respect the client has for your position (the used car salesman analogy). If a customer thinks you are just trying

to get a sale and forcing it within an unnatural timeframe for your benefit, they will lose trust in you and your process. While a "blue light special" may save them a couple of points and get you a quick sale, you've just lost any power you had to negotiate in the future and set the table for your competitors to take a more consultative approach. Sales reps are always under tremendous time pressures (revenue commitments, month-ends, quarter-ends, year-ends) but customers don't want to feel that your next meal hinges on their purchase. (What does it say about your offering if you are that desperate for a sale?) Great reps understand how to use time as a tool. Great leaders understand this principle and embrace the natural sales cycle.

2. Value: Using time to demonstrate value can be a critical way to differentiate your offering. If a customer truly sees value in what you are selling, they will go to great lengths to obtain it. The primary job of a sales rep is to align the value of their product, solution or service to the customer's requirements and reach a mutual understanding of the problem they are solving and the value

derived from the transaction. If value has not been demonstrated then time will certainly kill the deal. A customer who does not understand or share in your value proposition will grow uncertain and second-guess their purchase, providing your competition with an opportunity to establish trust and credibility over time.

3. Growth: If you accept the idea that trust and value can grow over time, then you will understand that clients will pay a premium for your product or service. If you are truly positioning a differentiated and shared value proposition to your client, they will look for ways to do more with you, ultimately leading to more engagements and more revenue. Avoiding "blue light specials" and "fire sales" will also serve to retain value in your offering and prevent future price deterioration; this puts you in a position of power when it comes time to negotiate.

As consumption models change, sales will need to adapt. These theories are great on paper but if you've got two days to close a deal at the risk of losing your job, then you are left with little choice but to force a sale. The next wave of sales leadership will understand the value of time and embrace the natural process, allowing customers to reach a buying decision, share in your value proposition and establish long term trust.

RUNNING, BEARDS & QUARANTINE: WHAT I LEARNED ABOUT GOAL SETTING (WHILE AT HOME)

Originally published May 13, 2020, on LinkedIn.com

I feel fortunate and grateful.

Fortunate to have a healthy family who can work and learn remotely, fortunate for employment, friendship, food and shelter.

Grateful for the people working on the front lines: teachers, first responders, healthcare workers, grocery store cashiers and many more. They have all proven to be the driving force and fundamentally underappreciated glue that binds our society, economy and national morale.

People across the planet have been totally devastated by this pandemic; it has forced us to re-assess and re-prioritize our lives. Beyond the physiological destruction caused by this virus, the psychological aspects of an abrupt disturbance to an established routine (paired with the ever-looming threat of fatal contagion from an invisible enemy) can have devastating consequences on our mental health. We all miss different things; seeing our loved ones, organized sports, going to restaurants, traveling, working with coworkers in an office or just the simple pleasure of going to a supermarket with an unmasked face to peruse the wide array of toilet paper.

The official start date of this pandemic is debatable but for me it began when I had to cancel a large in-person meeting in New York City on March 18th and on the same day cancel a family trip to Disney World that had been in the works for over a year. Canceling events are trivial inconveniences but for me it marked the end of normalcy and the start of something quite different, the "new normal." That weekend, like so many others, we were forced to come to terms with the new stay at home orders and this "new normal."

At the time of writing this, we are on day 56 (by my count) of quarantine and quite far from "normal."

The first Monday of quarantine felt strange. For the past decade I had been going through an unconscious (and comfortable) Monday routine. Sunday night: review the numbers and prep my presentations for Monday. 5:30 AM Monday: alarm goes off, jump in the shower, get dressed, feed the pets, black coffee in a travel mug and in the car by 6:15 for my 60–90-minute (depending on traffic) commute to midtown Manhattan. The rest of the week would unfold as usual: travel to various patches within the region, meetings, customers, partners, prospects, internal discussions, bench building, recruiting, interviews, pipeline development, operational checks, deal closings, celebratory dinners and so on until Sunday came around again.

If I had enough energy at the end of each day, I would hit the treadmill before helping with homework, dinner, more time with family and eventually catching some sleep.

At the end of the first Monday under quarantine, it hit me: I had allowed myself to become a creature of habit; my old routines had been rudely broken by a pandemic and there was absolutely nothing I could do to bring them back. It was time to break old routines and find a new way. I didn't want to wait for somebody to dictate my "new normal" and there were big things happening around me that were totally outside of my control (economy, jobs, travel restrictions) so I decided to write down my "quarantine goals" and take back some semblance of control over my personal life. It turns out that my brain enjoys routine, consistency and the feeling of control over small things; setting time-bound and measurable goals had always motivated me to try and improve every day. It also gave me a small sense of control in an unpredictable world.

I was never much of a runner. In the time and place where I grew up (1980s blue-collar London), we didn't run unless we were being chased (which actually did happen on a few occasions). If you had extra time in your day for something as frivolous as recreational running, it was a sure sign that you should probably get a second job or find something more productive to do.

My perspective on running has evolved over time; I entered a charity 5K race a few years ago to support my son's school; I had zero training and definitely did not consider myself a runner, but I ran as fast and hard as I could for 3.1 miles until I felt dizzy and close to throwing up. I finished first place for my age group (in a small competitive field) and the wheels started turning: "Could I have done better if I trained? Could I run further if I tried? Should I invest in some real running shoes?" I loved the competitive aspect of running (me vs. my personal record and me vs. a bunch of strangers who probably run more than me). Running lends itself to goal setting. You can set a time-bound and measurable goal, see and feel the physical benefits of cardiovascular activity on your body and track your improvement over time. Over the next few years, I researched hydration strategies, fueling techniques, running gait, foot placement, posture, breathing, etc. and ran in dozens of 5Ks, some half marathons and even a couple of full marathons (NYC & NJ). My time was never impressive but I felt the improvement and enjoyed the competition...

When I decided to set quarantine goals that Monday, I decided on these three:

1. Replace your commute with a run and cover a distance of at least 5K every day. (Set a goal that is time bound and measurable.)

2. Don't shave. Grow a big, ridiculous beard. (Regain a small sense of control.)

3. Be as self-reliant as possible. (Homemade food, etc.)

As we approach the 60th day of quarantine, I can say that I have achieved my first goal and established a new habit for the foreseeable future. I am running at least 5K every day (sometimes as far as 13 miles if I have the time and energy). During quarantine, I set a new personal record for a half marathon and a 5K. I can feel the improvement in my lung capacity; I've been able to tackle inclines with speeds that used to have me buckled over for air. This week I ran 7 uphill miles (at 7 mph). At the 1-hour mark my watch beeped to tell me that 60 minutes had elapsed; I felt like I could run forever (much better than I felt two months ago). It reminded me of a poster I saw somewhere (probably in a high school gym). It said something like, "It's not getting easier, you're getting stronger."

As far as my second goal, I did manage to grow a big, ridiculous beard and although it adds some wind resistance to my runs, I'm getting used to it and I don't hate how it looks. I was recently challenged by a coworker to keep it until Christmas for a "beard-off." (He has a well-established and formidable Santa beard.) I accepted his challenge.

When it comes to being more self-reliant, I did bake some French bread during quarantine with edible results and I've been helping my wife in the garden to grow some of our favorite produce. Not sure I'll be a baker anytime soon but I do have a newfound respect for the people and processes involved in the production of a crusty ciabatta loaf.

This isn't about running, this isn't about sports, and it's certainly not about beards or bread making. For me, this quarantine has presented an opportunity to re-focus on daily gratitude, self-improvement and the importance of goal setting.

Many of us will emerge from this pandemic and it will be a small footnote in history. So many others are not as fortunate. I hope as a society we do not forget the sacrifices that were made during this time by so many brave souls and I hope that we will remember to appreciate even the small things (like an abundance of toilet paper).

WHY I STARTED PUTTING MY PHONE FACE-DOWN DURING ZOOM MEETINGS

Originally published April 22, 2021, on LinkedIn.com

It's been over a year since I've set foot in a customer's office. Like most people, I've been in countless meetings over the decades; most of them in New York City and the meeting ritual is always the same:

Enter the lobby, get on the security line, exchange pleasantries with the guard, have your picture taken, stick the temporary badge to your suit jacket, navigate the elevator system, head upstairs, greet the person at the front desk, decline their polite offer for water or coffee, conduct last minute prep with the team and then wait in the lobby for the customer's arrival. Eventually, we would find our way to the conference room, unveil a peace offering of freshly made bagels or donuts from the coffee shop downstairs, strategically choose a chair, open a notebook to a fresh page and most importantly silence our phones and place them face-down on the table before getting down to business.

There's a long list of socially agreed upon politeness cues and 'Body English' in western business culture by which most people abide: eye contact, active listening, hand shaking, head nodding, good posture, etc. There is an equally long list of behaviors that are considered rude, like talking over people, not listening or checking emails during a meeting.

Being on Zoom and web meetings all day has changed our behaviors in myriad ways; some are positive and others have subtly crept in during the pandemic.

I was on a Zoom meeting last week and I noticed the person I was meeting with had darting eyes (it appeared they were looking at multiple screens). It felt like they weren't listening or at best half listening; it didn't feel great as the active speaker. It also occurred to me that I was guilty of no longer abiding by the unspoken code of meeting politeness to which I once strictly adhered. The webcam's limited field allows us to check emails or respond to texts out of view from our fellow meeting participants. During the pandemic, I have been multitasking off camera, prepping for my next calls and generally doing things that I would never do in person.

The pandemic has changed some aspects of business permanently (I don't think we will ever go back to shaking hands), but I do hope to be back in a customer lobby very soon. In the meantime, I'm going to change the way I Zoom. If you've been a victim of my distractions and multitasking over the past 12 months, I apologize, but you now have my full attention!

I may not have fresh donuts and a lightly starched French cuff shirt but my phone will be face-down, my email will be closed and I will be listening.

LIVE. WORK. SOBER.

Originally published June 22, 2022, on LinkedIn.com

The hardest thing about sobriety is figuring out what to do with all the extra time and energy.

Can I get an extra dirty, Grey Goose® martini, up with olives (blue cheese stuffed if you have them)?

Mmm. so good. Troubles drifting away, eyes glaze, smiling easy now.

Couple more please, carefree. Words flowing.

Great to see you, been so long. Where to next?

Bunch of apps for the table please, extra truffle fries.

I can dance.

Sorry, daddy has an event tonight.

Can I see your wine list?

Can't drive like this. Leave the car, find a hotel.

So tired, room spinning, where's my debit card?

3AM, heart racing, dry mouth, need water. Where am I?

What did I say?

Missed calls. God, what did I post?

Head pounding.

Need a toothbrush, I should be home.

Feel like shit, spent too much.

Need a shower, gotta get home.

Need a greasy breakfast.

I'm out of shape, need to work out.

So tired, need to stop.

Yeah man, I'm still good for Friday, looking forward to it.

Alcohol has always played a central role in my life. Growing up in the UK, family events were usually centered around drinking. Some of my fondest memories as a child involved spending time with my family and friends at pubs and in beer gardens.

As I grew older, my relationship with booze became more precarious.

I never considered myself an alcoholic but I would avoid certain restaurants that didn't have a bar and I would make plans around drinking. Plenty of poor and regretful decisions were made while under the influence, but some great times were also had. I pass zero judgment on people who can incorporate alcohol into their lives. Most people can drink responsibly and find a healthy balance of moderation. I struggle with moderation.

I will have a drink again, but not today.

About six months ago, I woke up in a hotel room in Costa Rica, sweating and somewhat panicked. I must have fallen asleep in the afternoon. Drinking in the sun all day catches up to you fast. Everyone's asleep, it's 2AM; what did I miss, I was wide awake, alone with my thoughts.

That was the moment for me. I decided it was time to try something new. Since I can't do anything in moderation, it was time to eliminate alcohol entirely.

Flying home, I was faced with my first challenge. I always have a pre-flight cocktail at the airport. Mimosa in the morning, bloody mary on the flight, nap it off and wake up at my destination. This time I'll have a coffee and a water.

The first couple of weeks were hard, incredibly hard. Cravings, temptations, doubts. Stick with it, keep your mind busy, find other things to do with your time.

After a few weeks, you are sleeping better, the cravings subside, you have more time, more energy.

Why didn't I do this sooner?

Waking up feeling refreshed, go for a run. Feeling light on my feet, will run a little further today.

Feeling energized. Happy.

Nighttime arrives, summer breeze, bistro lights; perfect night for a glass of wine on the deck under the stars. Don't do it, stay focused, you got this. Look at the stars through clear eyes; the earth is incredible. Work on your manuscript, stay busy.

Weeks turn into months, eyes are bright, skin is hydrated, anxiety has dissipated, sleeping solid, feel amazing.

So much extra time, hit the gym, re-visit your to do list, start a business, help others.

My son and his friends need picking up at 11PM, all the parents have been drinking and can't get them. I'm on my way, happy to do it!

I could get used to this.

I can drink whenever I want, but not today.

Since putting alcohol on the back burner my life has changed dramatically; in a relatively short period of time I've:

- Lost 25 pounds
- Eliminated hypertension and got my blood pressure under control
- Experienced zero heartburn
- Finished a manuscript (currently with the publisher)
- Joined a nonprofit board
- Started a business
- Monetized a YouTube channel
- Saved thousands of dollars on expensive wine
- Done countless late night sober dad taxi pickups for son and friends
- Been sleeping 8+ hours every night
- Had no hangovers
- Invited to more speaking engagements
- Increased amounts of energy
- Gone on longer and more frequent hikes with my dog, she is healthier

- Spent more time at home with family
- Started cooking healthier meals (no greasy breakfast sandwiches, no late-night drunk eating)
- Had no arguments
- Had no regrets
- Had no memory loss
- Increase in confidence

I'm not preaching. Do whatever works for you, but my experience was too drastic to not share. If my experience sounds hauntingly familiar and you are thinking about taking a break from alcohol, here are some things to keep in mind.

When you stop drinking, your brain will try to convince you to drink, keep the following list handy and refer to it when you feel like drinking.

Alcohol:
- Is expensive
- Causes anxiety
- Causes depression
- Causes insomnia
- Makes you say dumb shit
- Makes you eat like shit
- Makes you sleep like shit
- Is bad for your liver

- Is linked to cancer
- Makes you fat
- Makes you not sharp at work
- Ages your skin
- Gives you headaches and hangovers
- Dehydrates you
- Makes you self-centered
- Makes you lose self-awareness
- Lowers your inhibitions and makes you take greater risks
- Gives you acid reflux
- Increases blood pressure
- Erodes stomach lining
- Is bad for memory / sharpness
- Is bad for vision
- Means you can't drive / DUI
- Sets bad example for kids
- Gives you a disadvantage vs. nondrinkers
- Makes it harder to work out

A friend recently asked me to write up a realistic plan to ween off the booze, eat healthier, lose weight and get his life on track. Here is an 8-week plan that anyone can handle.

Eight Week "Back on Track" Plan

There are 3 issues you need to tackle:

1. Food
2. Exercise
3. Alcohol

Doing them all at once is extremely hard and will usually end in failure after a few days. Here is a realistic plan that will get you happy, sleeping better, less anxious, more productive and physically fit in 60 days:

- **Week 1:** Eat what you want but not before 10AM and not after 6PM. Don't worry about exercise or booze yet.
- **Week 2:** Eat low fat low sugar low carb but not before 10AM and not after 6PM. Don't worry about exercise or booze yet.
- **Week 3:** Eat low fat low sugar low carb but not before 10AM and not after 6PM. Move rapidly 20 minutes a day (fast walk or jog). Don't worry about booze yet.
- **Week 4:** Eat low fat low sugar low carb but not before 10AM and not after 6PM. Move rapidly 20 minutes a day (fast walk or jog). No booze on weekdays (only Saturday and Sunday).

- **Week 5:** Eat low fat low sugar low carb but not before 10AM and not after 6PM. Move rapidly 30 minutes a day (jog or run). No booze on weekdays or Sundays (only Saturday).
- **Week 6:** Eat low fat low sugar low carb but not before 10AM and not after 6PM. Move rapidly 30 minutes a day (jog or run). No booze period. Say no to booze every day this week.
- **Week 7:** Eat low fat low sugar low carb but not before 10AM and not after 6PM. Move rapidly 30 minutes a day (jog or run). No booze period. Say no every day this week.
- **Week 8:** Eat low fat low sugar low carb but not before 10AM and not after 6PM. Move rapidly 30 minutes a day (jog or run). No booze period. Say no every day this week.

Next time you are at a work function or bar, order a club soda with a splash of cranberry. Nobody is thinking about what you are drinking, they are focused on themselves. If you look around you will notice for the first time that a lot of people are in the soda club with you.

Not drinking at certain events is hard. I've made it through St. Patrick's Day, a wedding, countless customer dinners and work events, Father's Day, birthdays. You can do anything if you want it badly enough.

This isn't a group thing, this isn't a 12 step thing, this isn't a religious thing—it's a health thing. Alcohol is one of the few drugs that if you don't do it, people assume you have a problem. I felt compelled to share my experience, I hope you found it helpful.

AdamApps.com

APPENDIX B

EXERCISES

When I read a book, I usually don't do the suggested exercises in the back unless the author makes it convenient for me. Therefore, on the following pages, I've included some blank exercises based on key lessons from the book; all you need is a pen.

EXERCISE 1

INTROSPECTION

Use the following pages to conduct a self-examination. Introspection will help you uncover the root of your motivations and behaviors.

- What is your earliest memory of being a leader?

- Remember a time you achieved something greater than you thought possible. What was your motivation? What inspired you?

EXERCISE 2

TOUCHSTONE LEADER

Write down ten words that you think best describe you:

1.	6.
2.	7.
3.	8.
4.	9.
5.	10.

Think of the person you most enjoy spending time with. Write down ten words that you think best describe that person:

1.	6.
2.	7.
3.	8.
4.	9.
5.	10.

Reflection: Which words do you have in common? Which words from your favorite person's list are most admirable? Which words would you hope that others would write down when thinking of you?

Action: Choose one word from your favorite person's list that is not on your list. Come up with five activities or actions that would help others think of you in this way.

EXERCISE 3

YOUR COMMUNICATION STYLE

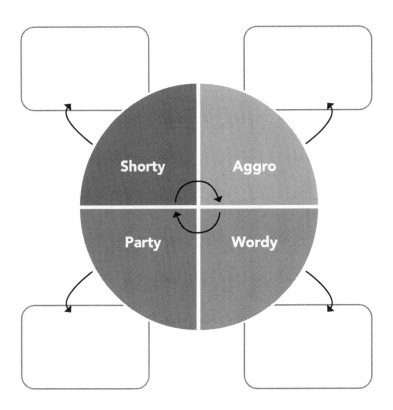

Write your name in the box you think best fits your communication style. Then think of five people whom you communicate with on a regular basis and write their names in the boxes that best fit their styles.

As a reminder:

- **Shorty:** To the point. Not a lot of details. Concise. Closest to Aggro. Opposite of Wordy.
- **Aggro:** Dominant. Aggressive. Loud. Closest to Shorty. Opposite of Party.
- **Wordy:** Lots of details. Analytical. Goes on tangents. Closest to Party. Opposite of Shorty.
- **Party:** Outgoing. Friendly. Emotional. Closest to Wordy. Opposite of Aggro.

Reflection: Is the person you have the most issues communicating with in the opposite quadrant? Do you share a quadrant with anyone and, if so, do you find that person easy to talk to?

Action: Choose somebody in the opposite quadrant (Wordy vs. Shorty or Aggro vs. Party) and write down five ways you can adapt your style to match that person's.

Name of person: _____

Next time you speak with the person, try using these five ways to flex toward their style. What do you notice?

1.

2.

3.

4.

5.

EXERCISE 4

YOU, THE LEADER

Answering the following questions will help you work toward establishing your identity as a leader. If you don't know the answers to some of these questions, think about the best leaders in your life. What qualities do they possess that you would like to emulate?

- What is your story (two minutes or fewer when spoken out loud)?

- Complete this sentence: I am great, but _____.

- What is your brand?

- What is your leadership philosophy?

- What are your core principles?

- What are your non-negotiables?

- What is your leadership style?

EXERCISE 5

SETTING GOALS AND TAKING ACTION

Complete the following questions to help clarify your goals.

- If you could remove all barriers and obstacles, what is the most grand and audacious vision of success you can conjure for your future?

- What action(s) would you need to take to make your vision a reality?

- What help would you need and from whom (specific names)?

- What immediate steps can you take to move toward achieving this goal?

- What are you waiting for?

EXERCISE 6

GIVING BACK

Who have you personally helped in your professional, personal, and family life?

NAME	HELP GIVEN	NEXT STEPS
Mr. Example	Gave him feedback	Mock interview

AUTHOR BIOGRAPHY

 Adam Apps currently serves as a Sales Leader for a Silicon Valley–based data management company. Adam has more than twenty years of experience working in high-tech sales and is recognized as an accomplished leader, career coach, mentor, and author. Adam has led teams at some of the largest tech companies in the world, like Cisco Systems, and has helped earlier-stage tech companies, like Pure Storage, transform underperforming teams into top-performing, cohesive units driving toward sustained double-digit growth. Adam serves as a nonprofit board member and holds his undergraduate degree in applied economics from Rutgers University.

Continue the conversation at *AdamApps.com* and on social media with the hashtag #ShittySalesLeaders.

Made in the USA
Monee, IL
14 April 2023

31831377R00146